Understanding Contract Law

Understanding Contract Law offers a clear introduction to the basic concepts of contract law in England. Built around familiar real-world examples that illustrate the concepts, principles and key cases upon which English contract law is structured, *Understanding Contract Law* is an ideal guide for those approaching an undergraduate law degree, or for general readers interested in this fundamental area of the law.

This concise, student-friendly overview, supported by chapter introductions and summaries throughout, covers the fundamental topics in English contract law, including:

- Agreement and Offer
- Acceptance
- Certainty
- Consideration
- Privity
- Misrepresentation

Max Young is Lecturer in Law at Waterford Institute of Technology, Ireland.

Understanding Contract Law

Max Young

Routledge·Cavendish
Taylor & Francis Group
LONDON AND NEW YORK

First edition published 2010 by Routledge-Cavendish
2 Park Square, Milton Park, Abingdon, Oxon OX14 4RN

Simultaneously published in the USA and Canada
by Routledge-Cavendish
270 Madison Avenue, New York, NY 10016

*Routledge-Cavendish is an imprint of the Taylor & Francis Group,
an informa business*

© 2010 Max Young

Typeset in Times by
RefineCatch Limited, Bungay, Suffolk
Printed and bound in Great Britain by
T.J. International, Padstow, Cornwall

British Library Cataloguing in Publication Data
A catalogue record for this book is available from the British Library

Library of Congress Cataloging-in-Publication Data
Young, Max.
    Understanding contract law / Max Young. — 1st ed.
        p. cm.
    Includes index.
    1. Contracts—England.   1. Title.
    KD1554.Y68 2010
    346.4202—dc22   2009022989

ISBN 10: 0–415–49425–7 (hbk)
ISBN 13: 978–0–415–49425–0 (hbk)

ISBN 10: 0–415–49426–5 (pbk)
ISBN 13: 978–0–415–49426–7 (pbk)

ISBN 10: 0–203–86423–9 (eBook)
ISBN 13: 978–0–203–86423–4 (eBook)

Contents

Table of cases

Table of statutes

Chapter 1

Introduction

CONTENTS

1.1 Introduction – what this book is about

This book is not intended to give a comprehensive coverage of contract law but it is intended to give you a good feel for the topic.

The book will, as far as possible, use examples that you would be familiar with in everyday situations. It will not go into complex contract situations such as purchases of land or houses (which lawyers call 'real property'); such areas of contract law are very specialized and are areas of law which are dealt with by lawyers as completely different topics.

The book will surprise you, I think, as to how often you enter into contracts on a daily basis without even knowing you're doing that.

The book will try and show you that contract law is not about 'having a good memory', but rather being able to grasp the legal principles and apply them to different situations.

The book will explain how contract law is the fundamental business legal subject. Not only is it obviously relevant to buying and selling goods and services, but it also underlies such areas of law as employment contracts.

An important point to remember when reading through this book is to remember that the parties to a contract, for example, a seller and a buyer, make 'the law' between themselves as regards their contract. There is, generally, no 'law of contract' that imposes on the parties as to what they should agree. This is unlike the 'criminal law' which imposes on people what they must, and must not, do. So if Robert agrees to sell his brand new car that is worth £30,000 to Jill for £10 then that's the contract between the two of them. The law will not interfere with that contract.

One other point to bear in mind when reading through the book is that most people think that there can't be a contract unless there is a signed document. Although many business contracts take the form of a signed document, many do not. How many orders for goods and services are made by telephone, email or on the worldwide web? Every time you go into a shop and buy goods you enter into a contract with the shop; do you ever sign a contract with the shop? Generally not, although when you buy goods on hire purchase you will sign a written contract.

1.2 Putting contract law in the context of English common law

Before starting to look at contract law we briefly need to look at the context in which contract law operates. The law referred to in this book is what is known as the 'English common law'. English common law forms the basis of the legal system in England and Wales (Scotland has its own legal system). English common law gave birth to legal systems around the world, namely Commonwealth countries such as Kenya, India and Canada. It also gave birth to the legal system of the USA (except Louisiana which adopted French law). Although all these countries now have their own developed legal systems, English common law, especially contract law, is still to be found at the heart of much of their own contract law.

1.3 What is common law?

The basis of English common law is that it has been made by the judges sitting in their various courts over the centuries applying their knowledge of previous cases (precedent), their knowledge of commerce and, to a certain extent, their common sense. To illustrate the longevity point, contract law lawyers still refer to **Pinnel's Case**, which was heard in the court of Common Pleas in 1601. Although the court of Common Pleas has long gone **Pinnel's Case** is still good law today and is regularly followed and referred to in the courts today. Even today the courts are still 'making the common law', although these days changes to the common law are normally brought about by Parliament amending or repealing the common law by Act of Parliament.

1.4 Precedent

Precedent is, at its simplest, one court following the decision of a previous court. We'll see this in operation when we examine contract law in more detail. However, precedent does take strong account of the hierarchical nature of the court structure. At the top of the structure is the House of Lords. All courts below the House of Lords must follow the decisions of the House of Lords. The Court immediately below the House of Lords is the Court of Appeal. The Court of Appeal must follow the decisions of the House of Lords. The Court of Appeal also follows its own decisions. Below the Court of Appeal is the High Court. The High Court must follow the decisions of both the House of Lords and the Court of Appeal. The High Court does not have to follow decisions of its own, although it will usually do so. At all levels of the hierarchy a court can hold that the facts of the case before it is fundamentally different from all previous cases. This is known as 'distinguishing' cases. In such an instance the court will decide the case on its own merits and the case will then become precedent for future courts.

1.5 An overview of contract law

The book deals with the following areas of contract law:

- Agreement, offer and acceptance
- Certainty
- Consideration
- Intention to create legal relations
- Variation of contracts
- Privity of contract
- Terms of the contract
- Exemption clauses
- Misrepresentation
- Remedies for breach of contract.

1.6 Agreement, offer and acceptance

Agreement, offer and acceptance together deal with the formation – the making – of contracts. Formation deals with such issues as when is the contract made? Where is the contract made (an ever important issue now that more goods are purchased over the worldwide web from abroad)? When is the order placed? When will the goods arrive?

Formation is also very important in business contracts. When a business, Business 'A', orders goods or services on its own standard form contract is the contract made on their terms? What if their supplier 'accepts' Business 'A's order on their own standard form contract? Now on whose terms is the contract made; Business A's terms or the supplier's terms?

1.7 Certainty of terms

Since the formation of a contract is all about agreement between the parties it is essential that both parties know exactly what has been agreed. This is where 'certainty of terms' comes in. 'Certainty of terms' deals with issues such as what is meant by ordering goods 'on the usual terms' from a regular supplier. What have the parties actually agreed? Are there regular terms between the parties? Are there different terms depending on what types of goods have been ordered? If the parties are not certain what they've agreed then there can be no contract between them.

1.8 Consideration and variation of contracts

Consideration and variation of contract terms are important and related features of English contract law. English contract law is based on the idea of a bargain. Both parties 'give' the other party something – the something is the consideration. Normally there is no problem in identifying what both parties give to the other. In a contract for the sale of goods one party gives the goods to the other party in exchange for the other party giving the seller money (the price). In such a case the seller's consideration to the buyer is the goods and the buyer's consideration to the seller is the money paid to the seller. However, what if you want to vary the terms of the original contract? This you can only do if you enter into a new contract which varies the terms of the original contract. In this case very often 'consideration' is missing from the new agreement. If this is the case you will be bound by the original contract.

For example, if you order 400 kettles from a supplier and then discover that you only need 200, can you 'cancel' 200 kettles?

Even if your supplier agrees can he later change his mind and make you take the whole 400?

1.9 Intention to create legal relations

When we look to see if a valid contract has been formed not only do we have to consider the formation of the contract and the presence of consideration, but we also have to consider if the parties to the agreement really intended to create legal relations (intended to be legally bound) to each other by way of contract.

1.10 Privity of contract

This area of law deals with the type of situation where you buy a holiday from a travel company for you and your family. If the holiday 'goes wrong', you can sue the travel company, but can the members of your family sue the travel company?

Another example. Assume that your company enters into a contract with another company. Say that under one of the terms of that contract the other company agrees to pay some money to 'your' company and some money direct to you in your own personal capacity. What happens if the other company then refuses to pay you? Can you sue the other company?

1.11 Terms of the contract

What do we mean by 'terms' of the contract? In the example above of Robert selling his brand new car that is worth £30,000 to Jill for £10 then the terms of the contract are Robert agreeing to sell his car to Jill for £10 and Jill agreeing to pay Robert the £10.

Other points to consider is how important are the terms of the contract? Are all the terms of equal importance? Can you break some terms but not others? Are the 'penalties' for breaking some terms less onerous than others?

1.12 Exclusion/exemption clauses

If the other party breaks a term of the contract can he escape liability because the contract contains a term which excludes his liability for that particular breach? Just suppose that the contract contains a term that says that if the other party does break a certain term then he will not be liable for that breach. This is what's known as an exclusion or exemption clause. Is it valid? This section on exemption clauses looks at the common law approach and the statutory approach to terms of the contract that purport to limit or exclude liability for breach of contract.

1.13 Misrepresentation

If a person sells you a second-hand car and tells you that he has owned it from new and it later turns out that it's been owned by 10 people, what are your remedies?

Has that person's statement been made a part of the contract, i.e. has it become a term of the contract? If it wasn't a term have you a remedy? Can you sue the seller for the false statement that he made to you?

1.14 Remedies for breach of contract

This section deals with what is meant by breach of contract and the effects of such a breach. Does every breach of contract entitle the innocent party to treat the contract as at an end if he so chooses or must he go on with the contract and settle for monetary compensation (damages)? This section will also examine the nature of penalty clauses in English contract law. Do they exist? Are they effective?

Chapter 2

Agreement and offer

2.1 Introduction

Agreement, offer and acceptance together deal with the formation – the making – of contracts. Although it is obvious that it is important to see that a contract has been formed, it is easy just to examine the mechanics of contract formation – the offer and the acceptance – and then forget the whole basis of contract law, that is, the agreement. This chapter will examine the importance of the concept of agreement. In examining the concept of agreement the intention of the parties will be closely analysed. Finally, as part of the examination of the intention of the parties we will distinguish between an invitation to treat and an offer.

2.2 Definition of a contract

A contract is an agreement (usually between two persons) giving rise to obligations on the part of both persons which are enforced or recognised by law.

Warning! Since, for the most part, the law of contract is a common law subject, do not take any definition you are given as the only definition. Treat the definitions as working definitions to help you analyse contract cases, etc.

NB The 'persons' mentioned above are usually referred to as 'parties' to the contract.

NB Generally speaking, an agreement is made when one person accepts an offer made by the other.

NB We talk about the parties to a contract as the offeror and the offeree; the offeror makes an offer to the offeree.

2.3 Agreement

Time and time again you will be brought back to the fact that the fundamental basis of contract law is the agreement of the contracting parties.

The thing that distinguishes the law of contract from other branches of law is that it does not lay down a number of rights and duties which the law will enforce. In other words the law of contract does not lay down a list of things that are legal or illegal, or things that must or must not be included in a contract.

The law of contract consists of a number of limiting principles, subject to which the parties may create rights and duties for themselves which the law will uphold.

The parties to a contract, in a sense, make the law for themselves: so long as they do not infringe some legal prohibition, they can make what rules they like in respect of the subject matter of their agreement, and the law will give effect to their decisions.

For example, if June says to Fred that he can buy her pen for £100 and he agrees there will be a legally enforceable contract between June and Fred. The fact that Fred may have been foolish in agreeing to buy a pen that is only worth £1 is irrelevant – the parties to the contract have agreed to the price of £100.

Whereas it is generally true that agreement is reached when one person accepts the offer of the other person – in other words there is an actual agreement between the two persons – this is subject to what's known as the rule in *Smith v Hughes*.

> In *Smith v Hughes* (1871), **Blackburn J** said:
> ... If, whatever a man's real intention may be, he so conducts himself that a reasonable man would believe that he was assenting to the terms proposed by the other party, and that other party upon that belief enters into the contract with him, the man thus conducting himself would be

equally bound as if he had intended to agree to the other party's terms . . .

The rule in *Smith v Hughes* law establishes that the law is also concerned with the **objective** appearance of the agreement, as well as the actual fact, of agreement.

For example, if Freda makes an offer to John and John says that he accepts the offer, but secretly he doesn't intend to accept the offer, there is in fact not an agreement because in John's mind he is not really 'accepting' the offer; he is only pretending to accept the offer. However, to an outside person there would appear to be an agreement. In other words **objectively** there appears to be an agreement between Freda and John. In such a case the court would apply the principle in *Smith v Hughes* and hold (rule) that there was an agreement between Freda and John.

2.4 Offer

2.4.1 Definition of an offer

An offer is a proposition put by one person to another person made with the intention that it shall become legally binding as soon as the other person accepts it.

An offer may be made to an individual, or a group of persons, or to the world at large: see *Carlill v Carbolic Smoke Ball Co* (1893).

In this case the Carbolic Smoke Ball Company published an advertisement which read: '£100 reward will be paid by the Carbolic Smoke Ball Company to any person who contracts the influenza after having used the ball three times daily for two weeks according to the printed directions supplied with each ball. £1,000 is deposited with the Alliance Bank, showing our sincerity in the matter.' Mrs Carlill used the smoke ball as directed, but still caught the flu. She sued for the £100.

Bowen LJ said:
It was also said that the contract is made with 'all the world', that is, with everybody; and that you cannot contract with everybody. It is not a contract made with all the world. There is the fallacy of the argument. It is an offer made to all the world; and why should not an offer be made to all the world which is to ripen into a contract with anybody who comes forward and performs the condition? It is an offer to become liable to any one who, before it is retracted, performs the condition, and, although the offer is made to the world, the contract is made with that limited portion of the public who come forward and perform the condition on the faith of the advertisement.

2.5 Offer or invitation to treat?

In contract law we talk about '**offers**' and '**invitations to treat**' (or invitations to purchase).

Normally it is fairly easy to distinguish between an '**offer**' and an '**invitation to treat**', but sometimes it can be very difficult to distinguish between them. Basically it depends primarily on the intention with which a statement is made (remember throughout contract law we are always looking for the intention of the parties).

2.5.1 Definition of an invitation to treat

An invitation to treat is said to be a statement made by one person asking the other to make the first person an offer.

Sounds confusing doesn't it? Sometimes an invitation to treat is described as 'an offer to make an offer'. This is not really a very helpful way of describing an invitation to treat since an offer is a technical term in contract law and should only be used in its correct context.

Intention, as always, is the thing that distinguishes an offer from an invitation to treat.

If a proposition is made by one person with the intention that if the other party accepts that proposition there will then be a contract between them, then that proposition is an offer.

If a proposition is made by one person with the intention that if the other party accepts that proposition there will not be a contract between them at that stage, then that proposition is an invitation to treat.

What all this means is that you cannot 'accept' an invitation to treat.

2.5.2 Examples of invitation to treat

In the examples of invitations to treat that follow, consider carefully what proposition or factual situation made the court decide that it was an invitation to treat and not an offer.

Carefully identify the particular elements of the facts of the cases that persuaded the courts that what was intended by one of the parties was an invitation to treat and not an offer.

2.5.2.1 Goods on display in a supermarket

Pharmaceutical Society of Great Britain v Boots Cash Chemists (Southern) Ltd (1953)

Certain brand name medicines were displayed for sale in a self service store. The issue arose as to when and where the sale of the medicines took place. Was it when a customer put the medicines in her shopping basket or was it when she presented the goods to the cashier? The reason this was an important issue was because the **Pharmacy and Poisons Act 1933 s 18(1)** provided that it was unlawful to sell such medicines unless the 'sale is effected by, or under the supervision of, a registered pharmacist'. If the sale took place when the customer put the medicines in her shopping basket the sale would not take place 'under the supervision of, a registered pharmacist' because no pharmacist was present at that time. If, on the other hand, the sale took place when the customer presented the goods to the cashier the sale would take place 'under the supervision of, a registered pharmacist' because a pharmacist was present at the checkout desk.

So, the question before the court was when did the sale take place? Was it when the customer put the medicines in her shopping basket or was it when the customer presented the goods to the cashier?

The court **held** that the sale took place when the customer presented the goods to the cashier. The placing of the medicines in the shopping basket has no contractual significance. It was not even an invitation to treat since there had been no communication between the shopper and the shop.

Somervell LJ said:
One of the duties of the plaintiffs,[1] the Pharmaceutical Society is to take all reasonable steps to enforce the provisions of the Pharmacy and Poisons Act, 1933. The provision of that Act here in question is s 18(1).

The point which is taken by the plaintiffs is this. It is suggested that the purchase is complete if and when a customer going round the shelves in this shop of the defendants takes an article and puts it in the receptacle which he or she is carrying, and, therefore, when the customer comes to the pay desk, the registered pharmacist, even if he is so minded, has no power to say: 'This drug ought not to be sold to this customer.'

Whether the plaintiffs' contention is right depends on what are the legal implications of the arrangements in this shop. Is the invitation which is made to the customer to be regarded as an offer which is completed so that both sides are bound when the article is put into the receptacle, or is it to be regarded as a more organised way of doing what is already done in many types of shops – and a bookseller is, perhaps, the best example – namely, enabling customers to have free access to what is in the shop, to look at the different articles, and then, ultimately, having taken the one which they wish to buy, to come to the assistant and say: 'I want this'? Generally speaking, the assistant will say: 'that is all right', the

---

1 English law now uses the term 'claimant' instead of the term 'plaintiff'. The claimant is the person who sues the other party, the defendant.

money passes, and the transaction is completed' [I]n the case of the ordinary shop, although goods are displayed and it is intended that customers should go and choose what they want, the contract is not completed until the customer has indicated the article which he needs and the shopkeeper or someone on his behalf accepts that offer. Not till then is the contract completed, and, that being the normal position, I can see no reason for drawing any different inference from the arrangements which were made in the present case.

2.5.2.2 Goods on display in a shop window

Fisher v Bell (1960)

A shopkeeper was convicted of offering for sale a flick knife contrary to the Restriction of Offensive Weapons Act 1959 s 1(1); he had displayed the knife in his shop window. The shopkeeper appealed.

So, the question before the court was whether the shopkeeper was offering a flick knife for sale.

On appeal the shopkeeper was acquitted of 'offering' a flick knife for sale. Before the magistrates court he was actually convicted of 'offering' the knife for sale!

This case shows that goods on display are inviting customers to make an offer to buy them from the shopkeeper. In other words **'goods on display in a shop window' are an invitation to treat – not an offer to buy**.

> **Lord Parker CJ** said:
> The sole question is whether the exhibition of that knife in the window with the ticket constituted an offer for sale within the statute. I think that most lay people would be inclined to the view (as, indeed, I was myself when I first read these papers), that if a knife were displayed in a window like that with a price attached to it, it was nonsense to say that that was not offering it for sale. The knife is there inviting people to buy it, and in ordinary language it is for sale; but any statute must be looked at in the light of the general law of the country, for Parliament must be taken to know the general law. It is clear that, according to the ordinary law of contract, the display of an article with a price on it in a shop window is merely an invitation to treat. It is in no sense an offer for sale the acceptance of which constitutes a contract. That is clearly the general law of the country . . .

2.5.2.3 Advertisements in newspapers and magazines

Partridge v Crittenden (1968)

Partridge advertised Bramblefinch cocks, Bramblefinch hens, 25s each in a magazine called 'Cage and Aviary Birds'.

Under the **Protection of Birds Act 1954 s 6(1)** Partridge was charged and convicted of unlawfully offering for sale a bramblefinch hen contrary to Protection of Birds Act 1954.

Partridge appealed against his conviction.

Again, the question before the appeal court was whether Partridge had offered a bramblefinch hen for sale.

Partridge was successful in his appeal. This case shows that goods advertised in a newspaper or magazine are an 'invitation to treat'; the advertisements are inviting customers to make an offer to buy them from the advertiser.

> **Ashworth J** following precedent said:
> . . . Having been referred to the decision of this court in *Fisher v Bell* the justices nonetheless took the view that the advertisement did constitute an offer for sale . . . Before this court counsel for the appellant, has taken two points, first that this was not an offer for sale . . .
> . . . [T]he real point of substance in this case arose from the words 'offer for sale', and it is to be noted in s.6 of the Act of 1954 that the operative words are 'any person sells, offers for sale or has in his possession for sale'. For some reason which counsel for the respondent has not been able to explain, those responsible for the prosecution in this case chose, out of the trio of possible offences, the one which could not succeed. There was a sale here, in my view, because Mr Thompson sent his cheque and the bird was sent in reply; and a completed sale. On the evidence there was also a plain case of the appellant having in possession for sale this particular bird; but they chose to prosecute him for offering for sale, and they relied on the advertisement.
> A similar point arose before this court in 1960 dealing, it is true, with a different statute but with the same words, that is *Fisher v Bell*. The relevant words of the Act in that case were: 'Any person who offers for sale any knife.' . . .
> The words are the same here 'offer for sale', and in my judgement the law of the country is equally plain as it was in regard to articles in a shop window, namely that the insertion of an advertisement in the form adopted here under the title 'Classified Advertisements' is simply an invitation to treat . . .
> . . . For my part I would allow this appeal and quash the conviction.

2.5.2.4 TV advertisements: are they an offer?

For an amusing take on the offer/invitation to treat issue, have a look at the American case of *John Leonard v Pepsico Inc* (1999).

In this case Pepsi advertised on TV a Harrier jump jet for 7 million Pepsi Points. John Leonard tried to claim the Harrier by paying for it as permitted by Pepsi's rules.

Judge Wood held that the advertisement did not constitute an offer. He also held that no reasonable person would actually believe that it was a serious offer.

Full report, see: <*http://www.hss.caltech.edu/~alan/law33/Pepsi_case.pdf*>

Link to advertisement: <*http://video.google.com/videoplay?docid=295016640043159024*>

2.5.2.5 Tenders

An example of a tender is where a company advertises that it wants a new factory built. The advertisement asks those who are interested in bidding (tendering) for the job to send in a price for the job. That tender amounts to an offer by the bidder to build the new factory for that price. Being an offer the tender can then be accepted or rejected by the company who wants the new factory.

In legal jargon a tender is an offer in response to an invitation to tender put out by a company.

Generally a company who invites tenders is only treated as an invitation to treat and not an offer. Therefore, a company who invites tenders is not bound to accept any of the tenders.

Spencer v Harding (1870)

Harding sent out a circular which stated 'We are instructed to offer to the wholesale trade for sale by tender the stock in trade of Messrs. G. Eilbeck & Co. amounting as per stock-book to £2503 13s 1d, and which will be sold at a discount in one lot. Payment to be made in cash. The stock may be viewed on the premises, up to Thursday, the 20th instant, on which day, at 12 o'clock at noon precisely, the tenders will be received and opened at our offices.' Spencer claimed that the circular was an offer which he had accepted by submitting the highest tender.

So, the question before the court was whether Harding's circular amounted to a valid offer which Spencer had correctly accepted or nothing more than an. invitation to treat and was, therefore, incapable of being accepted by Spencer.

The court held that Harding's circular amounted to nothing more than an invitation to treat and was, therefore, incapable of being accepted by Spencer.

> **Willes J** said:
> I am of opinion that the defendants are entitled to judgment. The action is brought against persons who issued a circular offering a stock for sale by tender, to be sold at a discount in one lot. The plaintiffs sent in a tender which turned out to be the highest, but which was not accepted. They now insist that the circular amounts to a contract or promise to sell the goods to the highest bidder, that is, in this case, to the person who

should tender for them at the smallest rate of discount; and reliance is placed on the cases as to rewards offered for the discovery of an offender. In those cases, however, there never was any doubt that the advertisement amounted to a promise to pay the money to the person who first gave information. The difficulty suggested was that it was a contract with all the world. But that, of course, was soon overruled. It was an offer to become liable to any person who before the offer should be retracted would happen to be the person to fulfil the contract of which the advertisement was an offer or tender. That is not the sort of difficulty which presents itself here. If the circular had gone on, 'and we undertake to sell to the highest bidder,' the reward cases would have applied, and there would have been a good contract in respect of the persons. But the question is, whether there is here any offer to enter into a contract at all, or whether the circular amounts to anything more than a mere proclamation that the defendants are ready to chaffer for the sale of the goods, and to receive offers for the purchase of them. In advertisements for tenders for buildings it is not usual to say that the contract will be given to the lowest bidder, and it is not always that the contract is made with the lowest bidder. Here there is a total absence of any words to intimate that the highest bidder is to be the purchaser. It is a mere attempt to ascertain whether an offer can be obtained within such a margin as the sellers are willing to adopt.

2.5.2.6 Negotiating the sale of a house

Gibson v Manchester CC (1979) important case

Mr Gibson wished to purchase his council house from the Council. The Council sent him a letter which read:

> . . . I refer to your request for details of the cost of buying your Council house. The Corporation may be prepared to sell the house to you at the purchase price of £2,180.

Consider the words above. Do they amount to an offer or an invitation to treat or are they of no contractual significance?

The letter continued:

> If you wish to pay off some of the purchase price at the start and therefore require a mortgage for less than the amount quoted above, the monthly instalment will change; in these circumstances, I will supply new figures on request. The above repayment figures apply so long as the interest rate charged on home loans is $8\frac{1}{2}\%$. The interest rate will be subject to variation by the Corporation after giving not less than three months' written notice, and if it changes, there will be an adjustment to

the monthly instalment payable. This letter should not be regarded as a firm offer of a mortgage.

Consider the words above. Do they amount to an offer or an invitation to treat?

The letter continued:

If you would like to make formal application to buy your Council house, please complete the enclosed application form and return it to me as soon as possible.

Mr Gibson sent in an application and stated that he wished to buy the house.

Did Gibson's application amount to an offer or an acceptance?

Lord Diplock said:

. . . The only question in the appeal is of a kind with which the courts are very familiar. It is whether in the correspondence between the parties there can be found a legally enforceable contract for the sale by the Manchester Corporation to Mr Gibson of the dwelling-house of which he was the occupying tenant at the relevant time in 1971. That question is one that, in my view, can be answered by applying to the particular documents relied on by Mr Gibson as constituting the contract, well settled, indeed elementary, principles of English law . . .

I can see no reason in the instant case for departing from the conventional approach of looking at the handful of documents relied on as constituting the contract sued on and seeing whether on their true construction there is to be found in them a contractual offer by the council to sell the house to Mr Gibson and an acceptance of that offer by Mr Gibson.

My Lords, the words [The Corporation may be prepared to sell the house to you at the purchase price of £2,725 less 20 = £2,180 (freehold). 'If you would like to make formal application to buy your Council house, please complete the enclosed application form and return it to me as soon as possible.'] seem to me to make it quite impossible to construe this letter as a contractual offer capable of being converted into a legally enforceable open contract for the sale of land by Mr Gibson's written acceptance of it. The words 'may be prepared to sell' are fatal to this; so is the invitation, not, be it noted, to accept the offer, but 'to make formal application to buy' on the enclosed application form. It is a letter setting out the financial terms on which it may be the council would be prepared to consider a sale and purchase in due course.

2.6 Summary

In this section you've seen:

- the fundamental importance that 'agreement' plays in the formation of a contract.
- that a contract is formed when an offer is accepted.
- that not everything that seems to be an offer is an offer – it might be an invitation to treat.
- that a contract is an agreement (usually between two persons) giving rise to obligations on the part of both persons which are enforced or recognised by law.
- that generally speaking, an agreement is made when one person accepts an offer made by the other. However, this is subject to two qualifications that the law is also concerned with the objective appearance, as well as the actual fact, of agreement.
- that an offer is a proposition put by one person to another person made with the intention that it shall become legally binding as soon as it is accepted by the other person.
- that an invitation to treat is said to be a statement made by one person asking the other to make the first person an offer.
- that goods on display in a self-service shop are an invitation to treat: see *Pharmaceutical Society of Great Britain v Boots Cash Chemists (Southern) Ltd* (1953).
- that goods on display in a shop window are an invitation to treat: see *Fisher v Bell* (1960).
- that advertisements are an invitation to treat: see *Partridge v Crittenden* (1968).
- that words used do not necessarily make statement an offer: see *Spencer v Harding* (1870).

Chapter 3

Acceptance

3.1 Introduction

The previous chapter examined the importance of agreement and the role an offer played in the formation of a contract. This chapter considers the acceptance element in the formation of a contract. We will see that an acceptance is the unconditional consent to the terms of the offer. Bearing in mind the unconditional consent element of an acceptance we will, perhaps oddly it may seem, start by examining the contrast between an offer and what is known as a counter offer. The reason for this is that we will see that a counter offer has the effect of destroying the original offer. This being the case there is no longer an original offer left to accept. This chapter will also examine the general rules that determine when an offer has been accepted. The chapter will conclude with a consideration of the special rules that apply to acceptances sent by post.

3.2 Definition of an acceptance

Acceptance is the unconditional consent to the terms of the offer.

If an 'acceptance' contains any reservations, any variations to the terms in the offer, etc., then the 'acceptance' will be conditional. Since it will not be an unconditional consent to the terms of the offer it will not be an acceptance.

3.3 General rule

An acceptance has no effect until it is communicated to the offeror.

Entores Ltd v Miles Far East Corp (1955)

Miles Far East Corporation, a Dutch company, made an offer to supply cathodes to an English company, Entores Ltd. Entores Ltd made a counter offer to buy the cathodes at a price of £239 10s a ton. The offer was 'accepted' by Miles Far East Corporation sending a Telex from Holland. The issue before the court was 'Where was the contract made?'. This was important because Entores Ltd wished to sue Miles Far East Corporation in the English courts, but could only do so if the contract was made in England and not in Holland.

So, the question before the court was where was the contract made?

The court held that the contract was made in England. The court pointed out that an acceptance has no effect until it is communicated to the offeror. The telex was communicated when Entores received it and read it in England.

Denning LJ said:

This is an application for leave to serve notice of a writ out of the jurisdiction. The grounds are that the action is brought to recover damages for breach of a contract made within the jurisdiction.

When a contract is made by post it is clear law throughout the common law countries that the acceptance is complete as soon as the letter of acceptance is put into the post box, and that is the place where the contract is made. But there is no clear rule about contracts made by telephone or by Telex. Communications by these means are virtually instantaneous and stand on a different footing.

The problem can only be solved by going in stages. Let me first consider a case where two people make a contract by word of mouth in the presence of one another. Suppose, for instance, that I shout an offer to a man across a river or a courtyard but I do not hear his reply because it is drowned by an aircraft flying overhead. There is no contract at that moment. If he wishes to make a contract, he must wait till the aircraft is gone and then shout back his acceptance so that I can hear what he says. Not until I have his answer am I bound . . .

Now take a case where two people make a contract by telephone. Suppose, for instance, that I make an offer to a man by telephone and, in the middle of his reply, the line goes 'dead' so that I do not hear his words of acceptance. There is no contract at that moment. The other man may not know the precise moment when the line failed. But he will know that the telephone conversation was abruptly broken off, because people usually say something to signify the end of the conversation. If he wishes to make a contract, he must therefore get through again so as to make sure that I heard.

Lastly take the Telex. Suppose a clerk in a London office taps out on the teleprinter an offer which is immediately recorded on a teleprinter in a Manchester office, and a clerk at that end taps out an acceptance. If the line goes dead in the middle of the sentence of acceptance, the teleprinter motor will stop. There is then obviously no contract. The clerk at Manchester must get through again and send his complete sentence. But it may happen that the line does not go dead, yet the message does not get through to London. Thus the clerk at Manchester may tap out his message of acceptance and it will not be recorded in London because the ink at the London end fails or something of that kind. In that case the Manchester clerk will not know of the failure but the London clerk will know of it and will immediately send back a message' not receiving'. Then, when the fault is rectified, the Manchester clerk will repeat his message. Only then is there a contract. If he does not repeat it, there is no contract. It is not until his message is received that the contract is complete.

My conclusion is that the rule about instantaneous communications between the parties is different from the rule about the post. The contract is only complete when the acceptance is received by the offeror and the contract is made at the place where the acceptance is received . . .

Applying the principles which I have stated, I think that the contract in this case was made in London where the acceptance was received. It was therefore a proper case for service out of the jurisdiction.

3.4 Presumed communication

In certain exceptional circumstances the court will presume that an effective communication of the acceptance has taken place even though, in fact, the offeror has not read the acceptance.

Such a situation was explained by **Megaw LJ** in *The Brimnes* (1974), where he said:

. . . I think the principle which is relevant is this: if a notice arrives at the address of the person to be notified, at such a time and by such a means of communication that it would in the normal course of business come to the attention of that person on its arrival, that person cannot rely on some failure of himself or his servants to act in a normal businesslike manner in respect of taking cognisance of the communication, so as to postpone the effective time of the notice until some later time when it in fact came to his attention.

3.5 Silence is not consent

Because of the general rule that 'an acceptance has no effect until it is communicated to the offeror', it follows that if the offeree remains silent there will be no communication of the acceptance and therefore no contract will come into existence.

Felthouse v Bindley (1862)

Paul Felthouse wrote to his nephew John Felthouse offering to buy John's horse for £30 15s and added: 'If I hear no more about him, I consider the horse mine at £30 15s.' John never replied to the letter. By mistake the horse was sold by John's auctioneer, William Bindley, to a third party. Paul Felthouse brought an action in conversion against William Bindley. (The action was based on the claim by Paul Felthouse that the horse had been sold to him by his nephew and that therefore he was the owner of the horse and that William Bindley had wrongly sold his horse.) The court had to decide whether a contract had come into existence between John and Paul.

So, the question before the court was had John communicated his acceptance to Paul? If John had communicated his acceptance to Paul then there would be a contract between them and Bindley would not be able to buy the horse.

The court held that there had been no communication of John's acceptance to Paul before Bindley bought the horse and therefore no contract between them.

> **Willes J** said:
> [I]t is . . . clear that the uncle had no right to impose upon the nephew a sale of his horse for £30 15s unless he chose to comply with the condition of writing to repudiate the offer. The nephew might, no doubt, have bound his uncle to the bargain by writing to him: the uncle might also have retracted his offer at any time before acceptance. It stood an open offer: and so things remained until the 25th of February, when the nephew was about to sell his farming stock by auction . . . It is clear, therefore, that the nephew in his own mind intended his uncle to have the

horse at the price which he (the uncle) had named, – £30 15s. but he had not communicated such his intention to his uncle, or done anything to bind himself . . .

3.6 Offeree need not communicate acceptance

The general rule is that the acceptance (and revocation of an offer) **must be communicated**.

There is generally **no requirement that the offeree has to communicate** the acceptance or revocation.

3.7 Revocation of offer

The general rule is that an offer can be revoked (withdrawn) at any time before it is accepted.

(A promise to keep an offer open is not binding unless the offeror has provided consideration ('consideration' is explained in full later in the book).

Routledge v Grant (1828)

Grant wrote to Routledge offering to purchase the lease of his house. The offer was to remain open for six weeks. Grant then changed his mind about purchasing the lease and, within the six weeks, withdrew his offer. After Routledge had received Grant's letter withdrawing the offer he wrote to Grant, within the six weeks, accepting Grant's offer.

So, the question before the court was could Grant withdraw his offer within the six week period?

The court held that despite the fact that Grant had promised to keep his offer open for six weeks he was not bound to do so because there was **no** contract between himself and Routledge to keep the offer open for six weeks (this was because Routledge had not provided Grant with any consideration to keep the offer open for the six weeks). Thus, there being no contract between them, Grant could withdraw his offer by notifying (communicating) Routledge of the withdrawal of the offer.

> **Best CJ** said:
>
> . . . If a party make an offer and fix a period within which it is to be accepted or rejected by the person to whom it is made, though the latter may at any time within the stipulated period accept the offer, still the former may also at any time before it is accepted retract it; for to be valid, the contract must be mutual: both or neither of the parties must be bound by it . . .
>
> . . . So, on the same principle, it was decided in *Payne v Cave*, that a bidder at an auction may retract his bidding at any time before the hammer is down; and the Court said, 'The auctioneer is the agent

of the vendor, and the assent of both parties is necessary to make the contract binding; that is signified on the part of the seller by knocking down the hammer, which was not done here till the defendant had retracted . . . Every bidding is nothing more than an offer on one side till it is assented to. But, according to what is now contended for, one party would be bound by the offer, and the other not, which can never be allowed.' So, here, until both the plaintiff and defendant had agreed to the terms of the contract, either party had a right to repudiate it.

Dickinson v Dodds (1876)

On Wednesday 10 June 1874 Dodds signed and delivered to Dickinson a memorandum, which read:

> I hereby agree to sell to Mr George Dickinson the whole of the dwelling-houses, garden ground, stabling, and outbuildings thereto belonging, situate at Croft, belonging to me, for the sum of £800. As witness my hand this tenth day of June, 1874. £800. (Signed) John Dodds
>
> PS – This offer to be left over until Friday, 0900 hrs 12 June 1874. (Signed) J Dodds

So, the question before the court was whether the memorandum of 10 June was a concluded contract or an offer or an invitation to treat?

The court held that Dodds' memorandum was an offer. Despite the language used by Dodds, that is to say, 'I hereby agree to sell to Mr George Dickinson', Dodds' memorandum was an offer to sell his house to Dickinson.

Remember the test as to whether a statement is an offer, invitation to treat, etc. is the **intention** of the person making that statement.

It is clear from the words used by Dodds in his memorandum, that is to say, 'PS – This offer to be left over until Friday', that Dodds is only making an offer.

> **James LJ** said after referring to the document of 10 June 1874:
> The document, though beginning 'I hereby agree to sell,' was nothing but an offer, and was only intended to be an offer, for Dickinson himself tells us that he required time to consider whether be would enter into an agreement or not. Unless both parties had then agreed there was no concluded agreement then made; it was in effect and substance only an offer to sell. Dickinson, being minded not to complete the bargain at that time, added this memorandum – 'This offer to be left over until Friday, 9 o'clock am 12 June 1874.' That shows it was only an offer . . .

The next question the court had to decide in this case was that given that the memorandum was an offer was Dodds contractually bound to keep his offer open until 0900 hrs on 12 June?

The court held that despite the fact that Dodds said 'This offer to be left over until Friday, 0900 hrs 12 June 1874' there was no obligation for Dodds to keep his offer open until then; Dodds was not contractually bound to keep his offer open because there is no contract to this effect.

James LJ said:

... it is clear settled law, on one of the clearest principles of law, that this promise, being a mere nudum pactum [a promise not supported by consideration from the other party] was not binding, and that at any moment before a complete acceptance by Dickinson of the offer, Dodds was as free as Dickinson himself.

Dickinson v Dodds does not end there.

In the afternoon of Thursday 11 June Dickinson was informed by Berry that Dodds had been offering or agreeing to sell the property to Allan. Dickinson then went to the house of Mrs Burgess, the mother-in-law of Dodds, where he was then staying, and left with her a formal acceptance in writing of the offer to sell the property: this document never in fact reached Dodds, Mrs Burgess having forgotten to give it to him. In fact on Thursday 11 June Dodds had signed a formal contract for the sale of the property to Allan for £800, and had received from him a deposit of £40.

The court then had to decide was whether Dodds had withdrawn his offer before 0900 hrs on 12 June?

The court held that since Dodds was not contractually bound to keep his offer open until 0900 hrs on 12 June, he could withdraw it at any time before it was accepted.

The issue here was whether Dickinson knew that the offer was no longer open. Because Dickinson had been told by Berry that Dodds 'had been offering or agreeing to sell the property to Allan', the court held that Dickinson knew that Dodds was no longer intending to sell his house to Dickinson. Since he knew this there was no longer any offer left to accept.

James LJ said:
[I]t is said that the only mode in which Dodds could assert that freedom was by actually and distinctly saying to Dickinson, 'Now I withdraw my offer.' It appears to me that there is neither principle nor authority for the proposition that there must be an express and actual withdrawal of the offer, or what is called a retraction. It must, to constitute a contract, appear that the two minds were at one, at the same moment of time,

that is, that there was an offer continuing up to the time of the acceptance. If there was not such a continuing offer, then the acceptance comes to nothing . . . [I]n this case, beyond all question, Dickinson knew that Dodds was no longer minded to sell the property to him as plainly and clearly as if Dodds had told him in so many words, 'I withdraw the offer.' This is evident from Dickinson's own statements in the bill.

Dickinson says in effect that, having heard and knowing that Dodds was no longer minded to sell to him, and that he was selling or had sold to someone else, thinking that he could not in point of law withdraw his offer, meaning to fix him to it, and endeavouring to bind him, 'I went to the house where he was lodging, and saw his mother-in-law, and left with her an acceptance of the offer, knowing all the while that he had entirely changed his mind.' . . . It is to my mind quite clear that before there was any attempt at acceptance by Dickinson, he was perfectly well aware that Dodds had changed his mind, and that he had in fact agreed to sell the property to Allan. It is impossible, therefore, to say there was ever that existence of the same mind between the two parties which is essential in point of law to the making of an agreement. I am of opinion, therefore, that Dickinson has failed to prove that there was any binding contract between Dodds and himself.

3.8 Method of acceptance prescribed by offeror

An offeror can stipulate that an offer can only be accepted in a particular way.

For example, the offeror can stipulate that the acceptance has to be received by the offeror: see *Holwell Securities Ltd v Hughes* (1974).

NB *Holwell* is dealt with below under the topic: The postal rules.

3.9 Counter offer

A counter offer is a form of conditional acceptance because it contains different terms from those in the original offer.

A counter offer amounts to the original offeree telling the offeror that the offeror's original offer is unacceptable.

The effect of this is that a counter offer destroys the original offer.

In the following cases identify the offer, the counter offer and the acceptance.

Hyde v Wrench (1840)
On 6 June Wrench offered to sell his farm to Hyde for £1,000. Hyde offered to give Wrench £950 for the purchase of the farm, but Wrench wished to have a few days to consider. On 27 June Wrench wrote to Hyde stating he was sorry he could not feel disposed to accept his offer at present. On 29 June Hyde wrote to Wrench:

I beg to acknowledge the receipt of your letter of the 27th instant, informing me that you are not disposed to accept the sum of £950 for your farm at Luddenham. This being the case I at once agree to the terms on which you offered the farm, viz, £1000 . . . by your letter of the 6th instant. I shall be obliged by your instructing your solicitor to communicate with me without delay . . .

The issue before the court was whether there was a concluded contract between Hyde and Wrench. The court first had to consider whether Hýde's 'offer' to give Wrench £950 for the purchase of the farm it amounted to an invitation to treat or a request for information or a counter offer?

The court held that Hyde's 'offer' was, in fact, a counter offer.

We've seen that a counter offer **is a form of conditional acceptance** because it contains **different** terms from those in the original offer. The effect of this is that a counter offer **destroys** the original offer. Therefore, when Hyde offered to buy the farm for £950, he:

(1) rejected the original offer
(2) destroyed the original offer and
(3) made a new offer.

The court then had to decide was whether Hyde's letter to Wrench saying that since 'you are not disposed to accept the sum of £950 for your farm at Luddenham . . . I at once agree to the terms on which you offered the farm, viz, £1000 . . .' his letter amounted to an acceptance or an offer.

The court held that Hyde's letter was an offer.

We saw that Hyde's original letter amounted to a counter offer which **destroyed** Wrench's original offer. Since Wrench's original offer no longer exists – it's been destroyed – there is nothing for Hyde to accept! Therefore, Hyde's second letter is an offer to buy Wrench's land for £1,000. Wrench is then free to accept or reject that new offer.

Lord Langdale MR said:

. . . I think there exists no valid binding contract between the parties for the purchase of the property. [Wrench] offered to sell it for £1000, and if that had been at once unconditionally accepted, there would undoubtedly have been a perfect binding contract; instead of that, [Hyde] made an offer of his own, to purchase the property for £950, and he thereby rejected the offer previously made by [Wrench]. I think that it was not afterwards competent for him to revive the proposal of [Wrench], by tendering an acceptance of it; and that, therefore, there exists no obligation of any sort between the parties . . .

3.10 Battle of the forms

The following case is a classic 'battle of the forms' case. It shows how classic contract law is relevant and applicable to everyday business transactions.

Don't forget to identify the offer, the counter offer and the acceptance in the following case.

Butler Machine Tool Co Ltd v Ex-Cell-O Corp (England) Ltd (1979)

Butler Machine Tool Co Ltd quoted a price for a machine tool of £75,535 on 23 May 1969. Delivery was to be given in 10 months. On the back of the quotation there were terms and conditions which included a price variation clause which provided for an increase in the price if there was an increase in the costs. The machine tool was not delivered until November 1970. By that time costs had increased so the sellers claimed an additional sum of £2,892 as due to them under the price variation clause. The buyers, Ex-Cell-O Corp, rejected the excess charge. They said:

> We did not accept the sellers' quotation as it was. We gave an order for the self-same machine at the self-same price, but on the back of our order we had our own terms and conditions. Our terms and conditions did not contain any price variation clause.

The issue before the court was on whose terms was the contract made? Was it made on Butler Machine Tool's terms or Ex-Cell-O's terms?

The court held that the contract was made on Ex-Cell-O's terms.

Lawton LJ said:

The rules relating to a battle of [forms] of this kind have been known for the past 130-odd years . . .

When those rules are applied to this case, in my judgement, the answer is obvious. The sellers started by making an offer. That was in their quotation. The small print was headed by the following words:

'General. All orders are accepted only upon and subject to the terms set out in our quotation and the following conditions. These terms and conditions shall prevail over any terms and conditions in the Buyer's order.'

That offer was not accepted. The buyers were only prepared to have one of these very expensive machines on their own terms. Their terms had very material differences in them from the terms put forward by the sellers . . .

As I understand Hyde v Wrench . . . the consequence of placing the order in that way . . . was 'to kill the quotation'. It follows that the court has to look at what happened after the buyers made their counter-offer. By letter dated 4 June 1969 the sellers' acknowledged receipt of the counter-offer, and they went on in this way: 'Details of this order have been passed to our Halifax works for attention and a formal acknowledgement of order will follow in due course.' That is clearly a reference to the printed tear-off slip which was at the bottom of the buyers' counter-offer. By letter dated 5 June 1969 the sales office manager at the sellers' Halifax factory completed that tear-off slip and sent it back to the buyers.

It is true, as counsel for the sellers has reminded us, that the return of that printed slip was accompanied by a letter which had this sentence in it: 'This is being entered in accordance with our revised quotation of 23 May for delivery in 10/11 months.' . . . in a business sense, that refers to the quotation as to the price and the identity of the machine, and it does not bring into the contract the small print conditions on the back of the quotation. Those small print conditions had disappeared from the story. That was when the contract was made. At that date it was a fixed price contract without a price escalation clause.

As I pointed out in the course of argument to counsel for the sellers, if the letter of 5 June which accompanied the form acknowledging the terms which the buyers had specified had amounted to a counter-offer, then in my judgement the parties never were ad idem. It cannot be said that the buyers accepted the counter-offer by reason of the fact that ultimately they took physical delivery of the machine. By the time they took physical delivery of the machine, they had made it clear by correspondence that they were not accepting that there was any price escalation clause in any contract which they had made with the plaintiffs.

3.11 The postal rules – general rule

The postal rules **ONLY** apply **when the ACCEPTANCE is sent by post**.

General postal rule
Acceptance takes effect when letter is posted.

Adams v Lindsell (1818)
Lindsell, who were wool dealers, wrote to Adams, who were woollen manufacturers residing in Bromsgrove, Worcestershire, on Tuesday 2 September 1817, saying:

We now offer you eight hundred tods of wether fleeces, of a good fair quality of our country wool, at 35s. 6d. per tod, to be delivered at Leicester, and to be paid for by two months' bill in two months, and to be weighted up by your agent within fourteen days, receiving your answer in course of post.

This letter was misdirected by Lindsell, to Bromsgrove, Leicestershire, and as a result it was not received by Adams in Worcestershire till 7 pm on Friday 5 September. On that evening Adams posted a letter accepting Lindsell's offer.

The letter of acceptance was not received by Lindsell until Tuesday 9 September.

On Monday 8 September, Lindsell not having received an answer on Sunday 7 September, as they expected, sold the wool to another person.

The question before the court was when did Lindsell's offer take effect? Was it on 2 September when it was posted or on 5 September when it was received?

The court held that the offer took effect when it was communicated viz 5 September.

Remember that the Postal Rules **only** apply to the communication of postal **acceptances**.

The court then had to decide when Adams' acceptance took effect? Was it on 5 September when it was posted or on 9 September when it was finally received?

The court held that the acceptance took effect when it was posted, that is to say, on 5 September. This is because the Postal Rules apply to the communication of postal acceptances.

The final point for the court to consider was what was the effect of Lindsell selling the wool to a third party on 8 September? Did it bring Lindsell's offer to an end or did it amount to a breach of contract with Adams?

The court held that Lindsell's selling the wool to a third party on 8 September amounted to a breach of contract with Adams!

This is because the contract was formed on 5 September when Adams posted his letter of acceptance.

When Lindsell sold the goods he was, in fact, selling Adams' goods – not his own.

The selling of the goods by Lindsell to a third party did not bring his offer to an end since his offer had by that time been converted into a contract by Adams' acceptance of it. Because Lindsell has sold the goods to a third party he cannot now deliver the goods to Adams; he will, therefore, be liable to Adams for non-delivery of the goods.

Household Fire and Carriage Accident Insurance Co Ltd v Grant (1879)

On 30 September 1874 Grant applied by a letter for 100 shares (this was his offer to buy the shares) in the Household Fire and Carriage Accident Insurance Company Ltd. The shares were allotted to him (this was the company's decision to accept of his offer), and on 20 October 1874 a letter of allotment (the acceptance) was sent to him at the address given by him. Grant said that this letter of allotment never reached him and that he never heard anything about the shares until March 1877 when he received a letter demanding the payment of a call upon 100 shares (the shares had been issued partly paid and the 'call' was the demand by the company for Grant to pay the next instalment due on the shares). The jury found that the letter of allotment of 20 October 1874 had been posted, but that it had never been received by Grant.

The letter of acceptance having never reached Grant the court had to decide whether there was ever a contract between Grant and the company for the sale of the 100 shares.

The court held that there was a contract between them which had come into existence when the acceptance was posted on 20 October – the Postal Rules applied to the situation.

The fact that the letter never reached Grant was irrelevant. The contract was formed the letter was posted on 20 October.

Thesiger LJ said:
... How, then, are these elements of law to be harmonised in the case of contracts formed by correspondence through the post? I see no better mode than that of treating the Post-office as the agent for both parties, and it was so considered by Lord Romilly in Hebb's Case, where, in the course of his judgement, he said, 'Dunlop v Higgins decides that the posting of a letter accepting an offer constitutes a binding contract, but the reason of that is, that the Post-office is the common agent of both parties.' ... But if the Post-office be such common agent then it seems to me to follow, that as soon as the letter of acceptance is delivered to the Post-office the contract is made as complete and final, and absolutely binding, as if the acceptor had put his letter into the hands of a messenger sent by the offerer himself as his agent, to deliver the offer and receive the acceptance. What other principle can be adopted short of holding that the contract is not complete by acceptance until and except from the time that the letter containing the acceptance is delivered to the offerer, a principle which has been distinctly negatived? ...

An offerer, if he chooses, may always make the formation of the contract which he proposes dependent upon the actual communication to himself of the acceptance. If he trusts to the post, he trusts to a means of communication which, as a rule, does not fail and if no answer to his offer is received by him, and the matter is of importance to him, he can make enquiries of the person to whom his offer was addressed.

3.11.1 Possible to exclude postal rules

Holwell Securities Ltd v Hughes (1974)

On 19 October 1971 Hughes granted an option to Holwell Securities to purchase a certain property for £45,000. Clause 2 of the agreement provided: 'The said option shall be exercisable by notice in writing to Hughes at any time within six months from the date hereof . . .' On 14 April 1972 Holwell Securities' solicitors wrote to Hughes accepting his offer to sell his property.

The letter accepting Hughes's offer was lost in the post.

The question before the court was whether a contract had been formed when the letter was posted on 14 April?

The court held that **no** contract had been formed. You'd have expected that the court would have applied the Postal Rules to the situation, but instead the court held that the Postal Rules did **not** apply in this particular case.

> **Russell LJ** said:
>
> Holwell Securities' main contention [was that they had accepted Hughes's offer when they posted their letter of acceptance.]
>
> It is the law in the first place that prima facie acceptance of an offer must be communicated to the offeror. On this principle the law has engrafted a doctrine that, if in any given case the true view is that the parties contemplated that the postal service might be used for the purpose of forwarding an acceptance of the offer, committal of the acceptance in a regular manner to the postal service will be acceptance of the offer so as to constitute a contract, even if the letter goes astray and is lost. Nor, as was once suggested, are such cases limited to cases in which the offer has been made by post. In the present case, as I read a passage in the judgement below, Templeman J concluded that the parties here contemplated that the postal service might be used to communicate acceptance of the offer (by exercise of the option); and I agree with that.
>
> But that is not and cannot be the end of the matter. In any case, before one can find that the basic principle of the need for communication of acceptance to the offeror is displaced by this artificial concept of communication by the act of posting, it is necessary that the offer is in its terms consistent with such displacement and not one which by its terms points rather in the direction of actual communication.
>
> The relevant language here is, 'THE said option shall be exercisable by notice in writing to the Intending Vendor . . .', a very common phrase in an option agreement. There is, of course, nothing in that phrase to suggest that the notification to Hughes could not be made by post. But the requirement of 'notice . . . to', in my judgement, is language which should be taken expressly to assert the ordinary situation in law that acceptance requires to be communicated or notified to the offeror.

3.12 Summary

In this section you've seen:

* that an acceptance is the unconditional consent to the terms of the offer.
* that if an 'acceptance' contains any reservations, any variations to the terms in the offer, etc., then the 'acceptance' will be conditional. Since it

will not be an unconditional consent to the terms of the offer it will not be an acceptance.

- that a counter offer is a form of conditional acceptance because it contains different terms from those in the original offer. A counter offer amounts to the original offeree telling the offeror that the offeror's original offer is unacceptable. The effect of this is that a counter offer destroys the original offer: see *Hyde v Wrench* (1840).
- that an acceptance has no effect until it is communicated to the offeror: see *Entores Ltd v Miles Far East Corp* (1955).
- that silence is not consent: see *Felthouse v Bindley* (1862).
- that the offeree need not communicate acceptance: see *Dickinson v Dodds* (1876).
- that the offeror can stipulate that an offer can only be accepted in a particular way. For example, the offeror can stipulate that the acceptance has to be received by the offeror: see *Holwell Securities Ltd v Hughes* (1974).
- that the postal rules only apply when the acceptance is sent by post.
- that the acceptance takes effect when letter is posted: see *Adams v Lindsell* (1818) and *Household Insurance Co v Grant* (1879).
- that it is possible to exclude the postal rules. For example, the offeror can state in the offer that the acceptance has to be received by him: see *Holwell Securities Ltd v Hughes* (1974).
- that an offer can be withdrawn at any time before it is accepted.
- that an offer not terminated merely by acting inconsistently with it: see *Adams v Lindsell* (1818).
- that a promise to keep an offer open is not binding unless the offeror has provided consideration: see *Routledge v Grant* (1828).
- that an exception to the general rule that notice must be communicated to the offeree before it takes effect is estoppel: see *The Brimnes* (1974).
- that the offeror does not have to communicate the revocation in order that the revocation be effective – a third party can communicate the revocation: see *Dickinson v Dodds* (1876).

Chapter 4

Certainty

CONTENTS

4.1 Introduction

This chapter deals with certainty of terms. The general rule is that an agreement is not a binding contract if it lacks certainty. This takes us back to the fundamental principle of agreement. For a contract to exist there must be agreement between the parties. If the parties are not certain as to what they have agreed how can there be certainty in their agreement?

4.2 General rule

An agreement is not a binding contract if it lacks certainty.

An agreement will lack certainty either because it is too vague or because it is obviously incomplete.

The reason that there will be no contract between the parties goes back to the underlying principle that a contract is an agreement between the parties: if the agreement is vague or is not complete how can the parties say they have agreed? What have they agreed upon?

4.3 Vagueness

An agreement that is vague will lack certainty and will therefore not be a contract.

Scammell & Nephew Ltd v Ouston (1941)

Ouston agreed to buy a lorry from Scammell 'on hire purchase terms'. Before the hire purchase contract was entered into Ouston decided not to proceed with the purchase. Scammell sued Ouston for breach of contract and Ouston replied that there was no contract of sale because the agreement was void for uncertainty since the words 'on hire purchase terms' were too vague.

The question before the court was whether the expression 'on hire purchase terms' had a clear meaning which both Scammell and Ouston clearly understood to be the same thing.

The court held that since Scammell and Ouston were unable to agree upon the true construction of the expression 'on hire purchase terms', it was, therefore, impossible to conclude that a binding agreement has been established.

> **Viscount Maugham** said:
> In order to constitute a valid contract, the parties must so express themselves that their meaning can be determined with a reasonable degree of certainty. It is plain that, unless this can be done, it would be impossible to hold that the contracting parties had the same intention. In other words, the consensus ad idem would be a matter of mere conjecture.
>
> A hire-purchase agreement may assume many forms, and some of the variations in those forms are of the most important character – e.g., those which relate to termination of the agreement, warranty of fitness, duties as to repairs, interest, and so forth.
>
> Bearing these facts in mind, what do the words 'hire-purchase terms' mean in the present case? They may indicate that the hire-purchase agreement was to be granted by the appellants, or, on the other hand, by some finance company acting in collaboration with the appellants. They may contemplate that the appellants were to receive by installments a sum of £168 spread over a period of 2 years upon delivering the new van and receiving the old car, or, on the other hand, that the appellants were to receive from a third party a lump sum of £168, and that the third party, presumably a finance company, was to receive from the respondents a larger sum than £168, to include interest and profit spread over a period of 2 years. Moreover, nothing is said (except as to the 2-years' period) as to the terms of the hire-purchase agreement – for instance, as to the interest payable, and as to the rights of the letter, whoever he may

be, in the event of default by the respondents in payment of the install-
ments at the due dates. As regards the last matters, there was no evidence
to suggest that there are any well-known 'usual terms' in such a contract,
and I think that it is common knowledge that in fact many letters, though
by no means all of them, insist on terms which the legislature regards
as so unfair and unconscionable that it was recently found necessary
to deal with the matter in the Hire-Purchase Act, 1938. These, my Lords,
are very serious difficulties, and, when we find, as we do, in this curious
case, that the trial judge and the three Lords Justices, and even the two
counsel who addressed your Lordships for the respondents, were unable
to agree upon the true construction of the alleged agreement, it seems to
me that it is impossible to conclude that a binding agreement has been
established by the respondents . . .

4.4 Incomplete agreements

If vital terms (such as the price of the goods) are left to be agreed by
the parties there will be no contract: how can the parties say they have
agreed?

What have they agreed upon?

May & Butcher Ltd v The King (1934)

May & Butcher Ltd alleged that they had agreed with the Controller of the
Disposals Board for the purchase by them of all the tentage that might
become available in the United Kingdom for disposal up to 31 March 1923.
Clause 3 of the agreement stated 'The price or prices to be paid, and the date
or dates on which payment is to be made by the purchasers to the Commission for such old tentage shall be agreed upon from time to time between the
Commission and the purchasers as the quantities of the said old tentage
become available for disposal, and are offered to the purchasers by the Commission . . .' Clause 10 stated: 'It is understood that all disputes with reference to or arising out of this agreement will be submitted to arbitration in
accordance with the provisions of the Arbitration Act 1889'. The High Court
and Court of Appeal held that the agreement was not a contract, but merely a
series of clauses for adoption if and when contracts were made, because
the price, date of payment and period of delivery had still to be agreed; and
that the arbitration clause did not apply to differences of opinion upon these
questions. May & Butcher Ltd appealed.

The issue before the House of Lords was that although it appeared that
the agreement was too vague because the price had not been agreed between
the parties could this problem be overcome since the parties had agreed to
arbitrate in case of any problems?

The House of Lords agreed with the High Court and Court of Appeal that
no final agreement had been made.

Lord Buckmaster said:

In my opinion there never was a concluded contract between the parties. It has long been a well recognised principle of contract law that an agreement between two parties to enter into an agreement in which some critical part of the contract matter is left undetermined is no contract at all. It is of course perfectly possible for two people to contract that they will sign a document which contains all the relevant terms, but it is not open to them to agree that they will in the future agree upon a matter which is vital to the arrangement between them and has not yet been determined . . .

The next question is about the arbitration clause. The clause refers 'disputes with reference to or arising out of this agreement' to arbitration, but until the price has been fixed, the agreement is not there. The arbitration clause relates to the settlement of whatever may happen when the agreement has been completed and the parties are regularly bound. There is nothing in the arbitration clause to enable a contract to be made which in fact the original bargain has left quite open.

Foley v Classique Coaches Ltd (1934)

On 11 April 1930 Classique Coaches entered into a written agreement with Foley by which they agreed to buy petrol and/or oil exclusively from Foley. Clause 1 of the agreement stated: 'The vendor shall sell to the company and the company shall purchase from the vendor all petrol which shall be required by the company for the running of their said business at a price to be agreed by the parties in writing and from time to time.' Clause 8 stated: 'If any dispute or difference shall arise on the subject matter or construction of this agreement the same shall be submitted to arbitration in the usual way in accordance with the provisions of the Arbitration Act, 1889.' For the next three years Classique Coaches bought petrol from Foley without any problems. Disputes then arose which resulted in Classique Coaches declaring that they were not bound by the agreement of 11 April 1930.

The issue before the court was whether the agreement of 11 April 1930 constituted a concluded contract or was void for uncertainty.

The Court of Appeal held that although in *May & Butcher Ltd v The King* the House of Lords concluded that a contract **had not** been formed, in this case a contract **had** been formed and therefore the court could use one of the terms of that contract – the arbitration clause – to fix the price! Confusing isn't it! The law's sometimes like that.

Scrutton LJ said:

In the present case the parties obviously believed they had a contract and they acted for three years as if they had; they had an arbitration clause which relates to the subject matter of the agreement as to the supply of petrol, and it seems to me that this arbitration clause applies to any failure to agree as to the price. By analogy to the case of a tied house there is to be implied in this contract a term that the petrol shall be supplied at a reasonable price and shall be of reasonable quality. For these reasons I think the Lord Chief Justice was right in holding that there was an effective and enforceable contract, although as to the future no definite price had been agreed with regard to the petrol.

4.4.1 Agreements to agree / agreements to negotiate

If parties are still to agree to terms of the contract, or are still to negotiate terms of the contract, then there is not yet full and complete agreement between the parties and therefore there is no contract between the parties.

Lord Denning MR explained the above reasoning in *Courtney & Fairbairn v Tolaini Bros (Hotels) Ltd* (1975).

> **Lord Denning MR** said:
> If the law does not recognise a contract to enter into a contract (when there is a fundamental term yet to be agreed) it seems to me it cannot recognise a contract to negotiate. The reason is because it is too uncertain to have any binding force . . . It seems to me that a contract to negotiate, like a contract to enter into a contract, is not a contract known to the law . . . I think we must apply the general principle that when there is a fundamental matter left undecided and to be the subject of negotiation, there is no contract.

Where all of the main terms in a contract have been agreed, and the parties have agreed to be bound thereby, the fact that further terms must be agreed from time to time will not prevent there from being a concluded contract. The main way to get around 'the agreement to agree problem' is to include an arbitration in the contract. By this provision the parties agree – when they enter into the contract – that if later they cannot agree on a price then an independent third party will fix the price.

4.5 Summary

In this section you've seen:

- that an agreement is not a binding contract if it lacks certainty.
- that an agreement will lack certainty because it is too vague. An agreement that is vague will lack certainty and will therefore not be a contract: see *Scammell & Nephew Ltd v Ouston* (1941).
- that if vital terms (such as the price of the goods) are left to be agreed by the parties, there will be no contract: see *May & Butcher v The King* (1934).

- that if parties are still to agree to terms of the contract, or are still to negotiate terms of the contract, then there is not yet full and complete agreement between the parties and therefore there is no contract between the parties: see *Courtney & Fairbairn v Tolaini Bros (Hotels) Ltd* (1975).

Chapter 5

Consideration

5.1 Introduction

English contract law is based on the idea of a bargain. Both parties 'give' the other party something – the something is the consideration. Normally there is no problem in identifying what both parties give to the other. In a contract for the sale of goods one party gives the goods to the other party in exchange for the other party giving the seller money (the price). In such a case the seller's consideration to the buyer is the goods and the buyer's consideration to the seller is the money paid to the seller. As part of the examination of consideration this chapter will consider the benefit and detriment test used in determining whether the parties have both furnished consideration to each other. This chapter will also examine what constitutes a 'valuable' – valid – consideration. Finally, as part of the examination of what constitutes a valuable consideration, the significance of past consideration will be explored.

5.2 Definition

> Consideration is some detriment to the promisee (in that the promisee parts with something of value) OR some benefit to the promisor (in that the promisor receives value).

NB The promisee makes the promise to the promisor.

In English law a contract is considered to be a bargain. What this in effect means is that each party to the contract gives the other party something: for example, in contracts for the sale of goods money (something) will be exchanged for goods (something).

The 'something' that is given is referred to in English law as consideration.

If both parties do not furnish consideration (give each other something) the contract is said to lack consideration and therefore there is no contract.

NB Benefit and detriment are alternative ways of testing to see if one party has furnished consideration to the other party.

NB The **promise** to give the other party something: for example money, is treated as a valid consideration.

In fact virtually all contracts start off this way i.e. a promise in return for a promise.

For example, when I offer to sell you my car for £6,000 and you agree to it the contract is formed at that stage even though I've not delivered the car to you and you've not given me the money. At that stage the 'promise' to deliver and the 'promise' to pay are both considered valid forms of consideration.

5.2.1 Explanation of definition

Remember two points:

(1) Consideration is a detriment or a benefit.
(2) Both parties must furnish consideration to the other party.

Let's look at a sale of goods example. Let's say Fred sells a pen (goods) to Jane for £5 (the price).

Fred's consideration to Jane viewed as a detriment
Fred's consideration, the giving of the pen to Jane is a detriment to him (the promisee) in that he parts with something of value – the pen.

Alternatively, Fred's consideration to Jane viewed as a benefit
Fred's consideration, the giving of the pen to Jane is a benefit to her (the promisor) in that she receives something of value – the pen.

We can therefore say that Fred has furnished consideration to Jane.

Fred's consideration applying benefit/detriment test

Fred sells pen

Jane receives pen. This is a benefit to her.
Alternatively, Fred's parting with pen
is a detriment to him.

NB What we're looking at here is to see if Fred has furnished consideration. Although Jane gets a benefit, the benefit is Fred's consideration **to** Jane.

We now have to do the same exercise for Jane – to see if she has furnished consideration to Fred.

Jane's consideration to Fred viewed as a detriment
Jane's consideration, the giving of the money to Fred is a detriment to her (the promisee) in that she parts with something of value – the money.

Alternatively, Jane's consideration to Fred viewed as a benefit
Jane's consideration, the giving of the money to Fred is a benefit to him (the promisor) in that he receives something of value – the money.

We can therefore say that Jane has furnished consideration to Fred.

Jane's consideration applying benefit/detriment test

Fred receives £5. This is a benefit to him.
Alternatively, Jane's parting with £5
is a detriment to her.

Jane pays £5

NB What we're looking at here is to see if Jane has furnished consideration. Although Fred gets a benefit, the benefit is Jane's consideration **to** Fred.

5.3 What constitutes a valuable consideration?

We saw that the definition of consideration stated that 'consideration is some detriment to the promisee (in that he parts with something of value) **or** some benefit to the promisor (in that he receives value)'.

So what constitutes a valuable consideration?

In *Currie v Misa* (1875), **Lush J** said:

A valuable consideration, in the sense of the law, may consist either in some right, interest, profit or benefit occurring to the one party, or some forbearance, detriment, loss or responsibility given, suffered, or undertaken by the other.

When we look to see if both parties have furnished consideration we usually look to see if one party has paid the other party for goods or services. However, as the above quote shows, other things such as giving up the right to sue the other party can constitute a valuable consideration. This is because the giving up the right to sue is a detriment to the party giving up the right, and a benefit to the other party in that he will not now be sued.

5.4 Types of valuable consideration

This book is not going to delve into the niceties of what can, or cannot, be a valid consideration in English law. For the purposes of this book it is assumed that the consideration furnished by the contracting parties will be the money paid in return for the goods or services provided.

5.5 Consideration need not be adequate

Although both parties must furnish consideration, there is no requirement in English law that the bargain be a balanced one. If, for example, Fred sells his car worth £15,000 to Jane for £1, there will be a perfectly valid contract between them. Both parties will have agreed and both parties will have furnished consideration; therefore, there is a contract.

Bainbridge v Firmstone (1839)

Bainbridge, at the request of Firmstone, allowed Firmstone to weigh two of his boilers. Firmstone promised that he would, within a reasonable time after he had weighed the boilers, return the boilers in a perfect and complete condition. Firmstone took the boilers to pieces, weighed them and then refused to put them back together again. Bainbridge sued Firmstone for breach of his promise to return the boilers in a perfect and complete condition; Firmstone pleaded lack of consideration.

Patteson J

The consideration is, that [Bainbridge], at [Firmstone's] request consented to allow [Firmstone] to weigh the boilers. I suppose [Firmstone] thought he had some benefit; at any rate, there is a detriment to [Bainbridge] from his parting with the possession for even so short a time.

5.6 Past consideration

5.6.1 General rule

The consideration for a promise must be given in return for that promise.

Hence the maxim – past consideration is no consideration.

Consider this question. A window cleaner cleans Fred's windows without being asked to do so. Fred agrees to pay the window cleaner tomorrow for cleaning the windows. On returning to be paid Fred refuses to pay the window cleaner. Is there a contract between Fred and the window cleaner?

The correct answer is 'No'. The window cleaner has furnished no new consideration in return for Fred's promise to pay. The window cleaner's consideration is past consideration and therefore no consideration.

Roscorla v Thomas (1842) demonstrates the practical application of the past consideration principle.

Roscorla bought a horse from Thomas for £30. On the following day Thomas called on Roscorla for payment. Roscorla gave Thomas the £30 and in return Thomas gave Roscorla a memorandum which stated that 'I have this day sold to Roscorla a bay nag for £30 which I warrant not to exceed five years old, and to be sound in wind and limb, perfect in vision, and free from vice.' As it turned out the horse was very vicious and restive. Roscorla sued Thomas for breach of the warranty contained in the memorandum.

The question before the court was did the warranty form part of the contract?

The court held that since the warranty was not given at the time of making of the contract it was not a term of the contract for the sale of the horse. The only way Roscorla could enforce the warranty was to show that there was a second contract. Roscorla could show that Thomas had made a new promise – the warranty – but he could not show that HE had given any NEW PROMISE in return for Thomas's new promise. In other words Roscorla had provided no new consideration for Thomas's promise of the warranty.

5.7 Summary

In this section you've seen:

- that consideration is some detriment to the promisee (in that he parts with something of value) **or** some benefit to the promisor (in that he receives value).
- that benefit and detriment are alternative ways of testing to see if one party has furnished consideration to the other party.

- that consideration must move from the promisee: consideration does not need to move to the promisor.
- that the consideration for a promise must be given in return for that promise.
- that past consideration is no consideration.
- that 'A valuable consideration, in the sense of the law, may consist either in some right, interest, profit or benefit occurring to the one party, or some forbearance, detriment, loss or responsibility given, suffered, or undertaken by the other': see *Currie v Misa* (1875).
- that consideration need not be adequate: see *Bainbridge v Firmstone* (1839).

Chapter 6

Intention to create legal relations

CONTENTS

6.1 Introduction

When we look to see if a valid contract has been formed not only do we have to consider the formation of the contract – that is the offer and acceptance – and the presence of consideration, but we also have to consider if the parties to the agreement really intended to create legal relations (intended to be legally bound) to each other by way of contract. This is normally straight-forward in the case of commercial contracts, but agreements between friends and relatives can lead to problems. For instance, if one friend agrees to drive her friend to the airport provided her friend pays for the petrol and that friend agrees to so do, is there a contract between them? There appears to be an agreement which is supported by consideration, but is that enough to form a valid contract? Did the friends in those circumstances really intend to form a legally binding agreement?

6.2 Intention to create legal relations

General rule:

> An agreement which is supported by consideration is not binding as a contract if it was made without any intention of creating legal relations.

Again, we are back to intention. If the parties did not intend there to be a legal binding agreement between them, then although there may well be offer, acceptance and consideration present there will be no contract.

6.2.1 Social/domestic agreements and commercial agreements

Generally speaking we distinguish between social/domestic agreements and commercial agreements.

General rule:

> There are two presumptions; first, social/domestic agreements are not intended to be legally binding; second, commercial agreements are intended to be legally binding.

NB Both of these presumptions are rebuttable: in other words although the presumption is that social/domestic agreements are not intended to be legally binding, it is possible to show that the parties did intend, in a particular case, to make the agreement legally binding.

Similarly, although the presumption is that commercial agreements are intended to be legally binding, it is possible to show that the parties did intend, in a particular case, not to make the agreement legally binding.

6.2.2 Social and domestic agreements

Most social and domestic agreements do not amount to contracts because they are not intended to be legally binding.

6.2.2.1 Husband and wife

Since such a relationship is a domestic one the general rule applies and therefore agreements between husband and wife are not intended to be legally binding.

Balfour v Balfour (1919)

In November 1915 the Balfours returned from Ceylon on leave. When they were about to return to Ceylon Mrs Balfour decided to stay in England on her doctor's advice. As Mr Balfour was about to sail back to Ceylon he verbally promised to pay his wife £30 per month in maintenance until he returned. In July 1918 Mrs Balfour was divorced from her husband. Mrs Balfour then sued her husband on his promise to pay the £30 per month maintenance.

The issue before the court was whether there was a contract between the Balfours.

Atkin LJ

The defence of this action on the alleged contract is that the defendant, the husband, entered into no contract with his wife, and for the determination of that it is necessary to remember that there are agreements between parties which do not result in contracts within the meaning of that term in our law. The ordinary example is where two parties agree to take a walk together, or where there is an offer and an acceptance of hospitality. Nobody would suggest in ordinary circumstances that those agreements result in what we know as a contract, and one of the most usual forms of agreement which does not constitute a contract appears to me to be the arrangements which are made between husband and wife . . . I think, that such arrangements made between husband and wife . . . not contracts, and they are not contract because the parties did not intend that they should be attended by legal consequences.

Spellman v Spellman (1961)

Mr and Mrs Spellman's marriage was going through a bad patch. They thought that if they purchased a new car their relationship might improve. Mr Spellman purchased a new car on hire purchase and put his wife's name in the registration book. Mrs Spellman asked if the car was for her and Mr Spellman replied that it was. Within three weeks the parties again fell out and Mr Spellman left his wife taking the car with him.

The issue before the court was who owned the car; this depended on whether Mr and Mrs Spellman had entered into a legally binding contract; had they intended to create legal relations?

Danckwerts LJ

Another matter which brings me to the conclusion that the wife is not entitled to relief in the present case is the principle which has been discussed in such cases as *Balfour v Balfour*. The proper conclusion on all the evidence in the present case is that there was not any intention to create legal situations, but merely an informal dealing with the matter between the husband and wife which is common in daily life and which does not result in some legal transaction, but is merely a matter of convenience. Consequently it seems to me that this point is also fatal to the claim of the wife in the present case.

6.2.2.2 Possible to rebut the presumption

However, it is possible to rebut the presumption that a domestic relationship between husband and wife is not intended to be legally binding.

Merritt v Merritt (1970)

The facts are stated in the judgment of Lord Denning MR.

Lord Denning MR

Early in 1966 [Mr and Mrs Merritt] came to an agreement whereby [their] house was to be put in joint names. That was done. It reflected the legal position when a house is acquired by a husband and wife by financial contributions of each. But, unfortunately, about that time the husband formed an attachment for another woman. He left the house and went to live with her. The wife then pressed the husband for some arrangement to be made for the future. On 25th May, they talked it over in the husband's car. The husband said that he would make the wife a monthly payment of £40 and told her that out of it she would have to make the outstanding payments to the building society. There was only £180 outstanding. He handed over the building society's mortgage book to the wife. She was herself going out to work, earning net £7 10s a week. Before she left the car she insisted that he put down in writing a further agreement. It forms the subject of the present action. He wrote these words on a piece of paper:

'In consideration of the fact that you will pay all charges in connection with the house at 133, Clayton Road, Chessington, Surrey, until such time as the mortgage repayment has been completed, when the mortgage has been completed I will agree to transfer the property in to your sole ownership.

Signed. John B. Merritt 25.5.66.'

The wife took that paper away with her. She did, in fact, over the ensuing months pay off the balance of the mortgage, partly, maybe, out of the money the husband gave her, £40 a month, and partly out of her own earnings. When the mortgage had been paid off, he reduced the £40 a month to £25 a month.

The wife asked the husband to transfer the house into her sole owner-ship. He refused to do so. She brought an action in the Chancery Division for a declaration that the house should belong to her and for an order that he should make the conveyance. The judge, Stamp J, made the order; but the husband now appeals to this court.

The first point taken on his behalf by counsel for the husband was that the agreement was not intended to create legal relations. It was, he says, a family arrangement such as was considered by the court in *Balfour v Balfour* . . . So the wife could not sue on it. I do not think that those cases have any application here. The parties there were living together in amity. In such cases their domestic arrangements are ordinarily not intended to create legal relations. It is altogether different when the par-ties are not living in amity but are separated, or about to separate. They then bargain keenly. They do not rely on honourable understandings. They want everything cut and dried. It may safely be presumed that they intend to create legal relations.

6.2.2.3 Parent and child

Again since such a relationship is a domestic one the general rule applies and therefore agreements between parent and child are not intended to be legally binding.

Jones v Padavatton (1969)

Mrs Jones suggested to her daughter, Mrs Padavatton, then resident in the USA, that she should go to England and read for the English Bar. Mrs Padavatton was at first reluctant to do this since she had a good job in Washington DC. Mrs Jones offered her daughter $200 (£42) per month maintenance if she would read for the Bar. Mrs Padavatton accepted her mother's offer and started the Bar course in November 1962. Then in 1964 Mrs Jones offered to buy a house in London so that Mrs Padavatton and her son could live there and let off the rest of the house to tenants so that the tenants rents would provide maintenance for Mrs Padavatton in lieu of the £42 per month. In 1967 Mrs Jones claimed possession of the house from Mrs Padavatton; Mrs Padavatton claimed that Mrs Jones was bound by the two agreements.

The issue before the court was whether Mrs Jones and Mrs Padavatton had intended either, or both, of the agreements to be legally binding.

Danckwerts LJ

. . . two questions emerged for argument: (i) Were the arrangements (such as they were) intended to produce legally binding agreements, or were they simply family arrangements depending for their fulfilment on good faith and trust, and not legally enforceable by legal proceedings? . . .

Counsel for the daughter argued strenuously for the view that the parties intended to create legally binding contracts . . . Counsel for the mother argued for the contrary view that there were no binding obligations, and that if there were they were too uncertain for the court to enforce. His stand-by was *Balfour v Balfour* . . .

There is no doubt that this case is a most difficult one, but I have reached a conclusion that the present case is one of those family arrangements which depend on the good faith of the promises which are made and are not intended to be rigid, binding agreements. *Balfour v Balfour* was a case of husband and wife, but there is no doubt that the same principles apply to dealings between other relations, such as father and son and daughter and mother . . .

In the result, on this view, the daughter cannot resist the mother's rights as the owner of the house to the possession of which the mother is entitled . . .

6.2.2.4 Social agreements

Generally speaking the presumption for social agreements is the same as for domestic agreements, that is social agreements are not intended to be legally binding. However, it seems that in such circumstances it is easier to rebut the normal presumption.

Parker v Clark (1960)

Mr and Mrs Clark were an elderly couple. Mrs Parker was their niece. On 18 September 1955 Mr Clark proposed that the Parkers should join forces and live with them. Commander Parker said that it was a big thing and required much study. After thinking it over Commander Parker wrote to Mr Clark saying that if they went to live with the Clarks they would have to sell their house. On 25 September Mr Clark replied by letter, which stated: 'Many thanks for your letter. The major difficulty re what is to happen to your house can be solved by our leaving our house to you when we both pass away.' The Parkers accepted this offer, sold their house and on 1 March 1956 moved in with the Clarks. Eventually the Parkers and Clarks fell out and in December 1957 the Parkers moved out of the house. They sued the Clarks for breach of contract, claiming a third share of the house.

The issue before the court was whether the two families had intended to create a legal relationship.

Devlin J

The contract relied on by the plaintiffs is said to be contained in the defendants' letter of Sept. 25 and Commander Parker's acceptance thereof. In this part of the case, since Mr. Clark and Commander Parker were the contractual protagonists, it is convenient to refer to them simply as plaintiff and defendant. The defendant's first submission in answer to the claim is that the letters, construed in the light of the surrounding circumstances, show no intention to enter into a legal relationship or to make a binding contract. No doubt a proposal between relatives to share a house and a promise to make a bequest of it may very well amount to no more than a family arrangement of the type considered in *Balfour v Balfour* which the courts will not enforce. But there is equally no doubt that arrangements of this sort, and in particular a proposal to leave property in a will, can be the subject of a binding contract . . .

That is the principle which I apply here; and, indeed, a contract of marriage is not dissimilar to an agreement by two families to live together for the rest of their joint lives.

The question must, of course, depend on the intention of the parties to be inferred from the language which they use and from the circumstances in which they use it. On the plaintiff's side, I accept his evidence that he considered that he was making a binding contract . . . He is not, in my judgment, the sort of man who would 'think up' a legal action as an afterthought when he found that he was not getting what he wanted.

... If [the defendant] had thought that all that his letter involved was an amicable arrangement terminable at will, I cannot believe that he would not have enlightened the plaintiff and, as a cautious man himself, have warned him against the folly of what he was doing. I cannot believe either that the defendant really thought that the law would leave him at liberty, if he so chose, to tell the plaintiffs when they arrived that he had changed his mind, that they could take their furniture away and that he was indifferent whether they found anywhere else to live or not. Yet this is what the defence means. The defendant gave several answers which show that this was not really his state of mind. He said that the object of the letter was to induce the plaintiffs to come to Cramond; and he agreed also that he made the will in fulfilment of the promise. I am satisfied that an arrangement binding in law was intended by both sides.

Simpkins v Pays (1955)
Simpkins lived with Pays as her lodger. Every week they entered a newspaper competition and one week they won £750. Pays refused to pay Simpkins 'her share' of the winnings.

The issue before the court was whether there was a legally binding contract between Simpkins and Pays.

Sellers J
... I accept the plaintiff's evidence that ... what was said ... was: 'We will go shares', or words to that effect. Whether that was said by the plaintiff or by the defendant does not really matter. 'Shares' was the word used, and I do not think anything very much more specific was said. I think that that was the basis of the arrangement ...

... It may well be there are many family associations where some sort of rough and ready statement is made which would not, in a proper estimate of the circumstances, establish a contract which was contemplated to have legal consequences, but I do not so find here. I think that in the present case there was a mutuality in the arrangement between the parties. It was not very formal, but certainly it was, in effect, agreed that every week the forecast should go in in the name of the defendant, and that if there was success, no matter who won, all should share equally.

Gould v Gould (1969)
In May 1966 Mr Gould left his wife. He agreed to pay her £15 a week, but he qualified it by saying: '... so long as the business is OK', or 'so long as I can manage it'.

The issue before the court was whether that qualification meant that there was no enforceable agreement at all; did Mr and Mrs Gould intend to create a legal relationship?

Edmund Davies LJ

... There can be no doubt that husband and wife can enter into a contract which binds them in law ... But it is on the spouse asserting that such a contract has been entered into to prove that assertion ... In the general run of cases the inclination would be against inferring that spouses intended to create a legal relationship ... The evidence establishing such an intention, needs, in my judgment, to be clear and convincing.

... According to the wife, the husband promised to pay her £15 a week 'as long as he had it' and 'as long as the business was OK' ...

In my judgment those words import such uncertainty as to indicate strongly that legal relations were not contemplated ... I have come to the conclusion that all that occurred here was that the parties entered into a purely domestic arrangement not intended to have legally-binding force ...

6.2.3 Commercial agreements

In commercial agreements (or agreements at 'arm's length') the general rule is that such agreements are intended to be legally binding.

6.2.3.1 Possible to rebut the presumption

However, it is possible to rebut the presumption that commercial agreements are intended to be legally binding.

Jones v Vernon's Pools Ltd (1938)

Jones alleged that he had sent in his football pools coupon which had won him £2,137 14s 7d. Vernon's Pools denied that they had ever received his coupon. The coupon contained the words that any agreement entered into was 'binding in honour only'.

The issue before the court was whether Jones and Vernon's Pools had ever intended to enter into a legal relationship.

Atkinson J

When all is said and done this coupon is sent in on certain terms which are printed on the back of every coupon, and the plaintiff admits that he knew perfectly well what these rules were, and that he read them, and if anybody can understand them he can ...

This [coupon] purports to be an agreement ... which is merely to confer rights short of legal rights, rights which cannot be enforced at law. The very first condition is this:

'This coupon is an entry form containing the conditions on which it may be completed and submitted to us and on which alone we are prepared to receive and, if we think fit, to accept it as an entry.'

In other words, it is making quite clear that these conditions which follow govern the whole relationship between the defendants and anybody sending in coupons. Secondly:

'It is a basic condition of the sending in and the acceptance of this coupon that it is intended and agreed that the conduct of the pools and everything done in connection therewith and all arrangements relating thereto (whether mentioned in these rules or to be implied) and this coupon and any agreement or transaction entered into or payment made by or under it shall not be attended by or give rise to any legal relationship, rights, duties or consequences whatsoever or be legally enforceable or the subject of litigation, but such arrangements, agreements and transactions are binding in honour only.'

That is a clause which seems to me to express in the fullest and clearest way that everything that follows in these rules is subject to that basic or overriding condition that everything that is promised, every statement made with relation to what a person sending the coupon may expect, or may be entitled to, is governed by that clause.

If it means what I think that they intend it to mean, and what certainly everybody who sent a coupon and who took the trouble to read it would understand, it means that they all trusted to the defendants' honour, and to the care they took, and that they fully understood that there should be no claim possible in respect of the transactions.

Rose & Frank Co v JR Crompton and Bros Ltd (1925)

Two English companies entered into an agreement with an American company whereby the American company would be their sole agent for three years subject to six months notice. The written agreement between the parties stated: 'This arrangement is not entered into, nor is this memorandum written, as a formal or legal agreement, and shall not be subject to legal jurisdiction in the Law Courts either of the United States or England, but it is only a definite expression and record of the purpose and intention of the three parties concerned, to which they each honourably pledge themselves, with the fullest confidence – based on past business with each other – that it will be carried through by each of the three parties with mutual loyalty and friendly co-operation.' A dispute having arisen between the English companies and the American company the English companies cancelled their agreement with the American company without notice. The American company sued the English companies for breach of the agreement.

The issue before the court was whether the main agreement was a legally binding contract between the parties.

Lord Phillimore

I was for a time impressed by the suggestion that as complete legal rights had been created by the earlier part of the document in question, any subsequent clause nullifying those rights ought to be regarded as repugnant and ought to be rejected . . . It is true that when the tribunal has before it for construction an instrument which unquestionably creates a legal interest, and the dispute is only as to the quality and extent of that interest, then later repugnant clauses in the instrument cutting down that interest which the earlier part of it has given are to be rejected, but this doctrine does not apply when the question is whether it is intended to create any legal interest at all. Here, I think, the overriding clause in the document is that which provides that it is to be a contract of honour only and unenforceable at law.

6.3 Summary

In this section you've seen:

- that if the parties did not intend there to be a legal binding agreement between them, then although there may well be offer, acceptance and consideration present there will be no contract: see *Balfour v Balfour* (1919).
- that generally speaking we distinguish between social/domestic agreements and commercial agreements. There are two presumptions:
  - ○ social/domestic agreements are not intended to be legally binding; and
  - ○ commercial agreements are intended to be legally binding.
- that both the above presumptions are rebuttable: in other words although the presumption is that social/domestic agreements are not intended to be legally binding it is possible to show that the parties did intend, in a particular case, to make the agreement legally binding.
- that similarly with commercial agreements it is possible to show that the parties did intend not to make the agreement legally binding.
- that social and domestic agreements generally do not amount to contracts because they are not intended to be legally binding. However, the presumption can be rebutted: see *Parker v Clark* (1960) and *Simpkins v Pays* (1955).
- that since a husband and wife relationship is a domestic one the general rule applies and therefore agreements between husband and wife are not intended to be legally binding: see *Balfour v Balfour* (1919).
- that it is possible to rebut the above presumption: see *Merritt v Merritt* (1970).
- that social and domestic agreements generally do not amount to contracts because they are not intended to be legally binding.

- that since a parent and child relationship is a domestic one the general rule applies and therefore agreements between parent and child are not intended to be legally binding: see *Jones v Padavatton* (1969).
- that in commercial agreements (or agreements at 'arm's length') the general rule applies and therefore such agreements are intended to be legally binding.

However, the presumption can be rebutted: see *Rose & Frank Co v JR Crompton and Bros Ltd* (1925).

Chapter 7

Variation of contracts

CONTENTS	

7.1 Introduction

Sometimes, parties who have entered into a contract find that they want to vary the terms of that contract for whatever reason. In such a case it is important to look back at the topic of consideration. Say, one of the parties agrees to pay more than the original price; is that party bound by that new promise to pay the higher price? Our study of consideration would say that the party agreeing to pay the higher price has furnished new consideration but has not received any new consideration. In such a case there is no new contract to pay the higher price. There is a new agreement, but that new agreement is not supported by fresh consideration. This chapter explains how parties to a contract can vary the terms of the original contract so as to make the new contract binding on both parties.

7.2 Contract variation

In the vast majority of cases once parties have entered into a contract the parties perform their obligations under the contract and the contract comes to an end – this is known as **discharge by performance**.

However, in some cases the parties wish to vary or change the terms of the contract. The simplest way in which the parties to the original contract can vary that contract is to enter into a **completely new contract** whereby they agree to vary the terms of the original contract – this is known as **variation**.

Alternatively, the parties may agree to abandon the original contract completely – this is known as rescinding the contract.

In either case provided both parties have **agreed** (offer and acceptance) to the new terms and provided that both parties have provided **fresh consideration** then there will be a new contract which either varies the terms of the original contract or rescinds it.

However, two problems may arise in this type of situation.

What have the parties **actually agreed**?

More usually the problem, what **fresh consideration** have both parties furnished?

7.2.1 Have both parties furnished fresh consideration?

Very often when parties agree to vary the terms of a contract what happens is that one party agrees to give up some right under the contract, but the other party does not. A common example of this is part payment of a debt.

For example, if Eric already owes Kate £300 and says to her 'Will you accept £200 in full settlement and forgo the remaining £100' and Kate agrees, can Kate, once she has got the £200 from Eric, sue him for the remaining £100?

In contract law jargon if one party is already bound by contract to pay the other party, is a promise by him to pay a lesser sum in full settlement good consideration? In other words what fresh – new – consideration do both parties agree to provide for the new agreement?

In the following case identify the new agreement; and then look to see what new consideration both parties agreed to provide – in other words what new consideration are both parties going to provide beyond that which they originally had agreed to provide.

Stilk v Myrick (1809)

In the course of the voyage two seamen deserted a ship. The captain, being unable to find replacements for the deserters, entered into an agreement with the rest of the crew whereby the deserters' wages would be divided equally between the remaining crew. On the ship's return to London the captain refused to pay the promised extra wages claiming that the remaining crew had not provided any new consideration.

The first point the court had to consider was whether there was a new agreement between the captain and the crew. The court held that there was a new agreement.

The next point the court had to consider was whether the captain offered the crew fresh consideration. The court held that the captain had offered the crew fresh consideration. The captain's fresh consideration to the crew was that 'the deserters' wages would be divided equally between the remaining crew'.

The next point the court had to consider was whether the crew had offered the captain fresh consideration. The court held that the crew had offered no new consideration in return for the captain's new promise to pay extra money. All the crew agreed to do was what they were obliged to do already. They had offered nothing new (that is, they had offered no new/fresh consideration).

Therefore, the court held that there was no new contract between the captain and his crew. Although there was a new agreement between the captain and the crew the crew had offered NO NEW CONSIDERATION in return for the captain's new promise to pay extra money. Since the crew has offered NO NEW CONSIDERATION, there is no new contract between them and the captain.

> **Lord Ellenborough** said:
> Here, I say, the agreement is void for want of consideration. There was no consideration for the ulterior pay promised to the mariners who remained with the ship. Before they sailed from London they had undertaken to do all that they could under all the emergencies of the voyage. They had sold all their services till the voyage should be completed. If they had been at liberty to quit the vessel at Cronstadt [where the desertion took place], the case would have been quite different; or if the captain had capriciously discharged the two men who were wanting, the others might not have been compellable to take the whole duty upon themselves, and their agreeing to do so might have been a sufficient consideration for the promise of an advance of wages. But the desertion of a part of the crew is to be considered an emergency of the voyage as much as their death, and those who remain are bound by the terms of their original contract to exert themselves to the utmost to bring the ship in safety to her destined port. Therefore, without looking to the policy of this agreement I think it is void for want of consideration, and that the plaintiff can only recover at the rate of £5 a month [their previous wages].

Stilk v Myrick remains good law – and it still is – but in 1990 in a landmark decision the law relating to the variation of contracts was revisited.

Williams v Roffey Bros & Nicholls (Contractors) Ltd (1990)

On 21 January 1986 Roffey and Williams entered into a written contract whereby Williams undertook to provide the labour for the carpentry work to 27 flats for a total price of £20,000. By 9 April 1986 Williams had completed the work to the roof, had carried out the first fix to all 27 flats, and had substantially completed the second fix to nine flats. By this date Roffey had made interim payments totalling £16,200. By the end of March 1986 Williams was in financial difficulty because the agreed price of £20,000 was too low to enable Williams to operate satisfactorily and at a profit (a reasonable price for the job would have been £23,783) and that he had failed to supervise his workmen adequately. Roffey were concerned that Williams would not complete his work on time and that they might incur penalties under the penalty clause in their main contract with the building owners. In order to make sure that Williams completed his work on time Roffey promised to pay Williams a further sum of £10,300, in addition to the £20,000, to be paid at the rate of £575 for each flat in which the carpentry work was completed. Williams and his men continued work on the flats until the end of May 1986. By that date Roffey, after their promise on 9 April 1986, had made only one further payment of £1,500. At the end of May Williams ceased work on the flats. Roffey therefore hired other carpenters to complete the work, but in the result incurred one week's time penalty in their contract with the building owners. Williams sued for the extra money that had been promised to him.

Roffey argued that their promise to pay an additional £10,300, at the rate of £575 per completed flat, was unenforceable since there was no consideration for it.

The question the court had to consider was whether Williams had furnished Roffey with fresh consideration? The court held that Williams had furnished Roffey with fresh consideration!

Although you might most reasonably have followed the decision in *Stilk v Myrick* the court held in this case that Roffey had received fresh consideration in the form of a BENEFIT!

The court said that the BENEFIT that Roffey had received was:

(1) the benefit that Williams continued work
(2) avoided the penalty for delay and
(3) avoided the trouble and expense of engaging other people to complete the carpentry work.

Glidewell LJ said:

Was there consideration for Roffey's promise made on 9 April 1986 to pay an additional price at the rate of £575 per completed flat?

In his address to us, counsel for the defendants outlined the benefits to the defendants which arose from their agreement to pay the additional £10,300 as (i) seeking to ensure that the plaintiff continued work and did not stop in breach of the subcontract (ii) avoiding the penalty for delay and (iii) avoiding the trouble and expense of engaging other people to complete the carpentry work.

Accordingly ... the present state of the law on this subject can be expressed in the following proposition: (i) if A has entered into a contract with B to do work for, or to supply goods or services to, B in return for payment by B and (ii) at some stage before A has completely performed his obligations under the contract B has reason to doubt whether A will, or will be able to, complete his side of the bargain and (iii) B thereupon promises A an additional payment in return for A's promise to perform his contractual obligations on time and (iv) as a result of giving his promise, B obtains in practice a benefit, or obviates a disbenefit, and (v) B's promise is not given as a result of economic duress or fraud on the part of A, then (vi) the benefit to B is capable of being consideration for B's promise, so that the promise will be legally binding.

NB *Williams v Roffey* does not overrule *Stilk v Myrick*, but it does indicate a practical businesslike way in which the rule in *Stilk v Myrick* can be overcome.

7.3 Summary

In this section you've seen:

- that the simplest way in which the parties to a contract can vary that contract is to enter into a completely new contract whereby they agree to vary the terms of the original contract.
- that in order to vary the terms of a contract, BOTH parties must furnish fresh (new) consideration.

Privity

CONTENTS

8.1 Introduction

This chapter will explain that generally speaking only the parties to a contract can be bound by it or derive benefits from it. It is only the parties to the contract that are privy to it. This is known as privity of contract. For example, what if you buy a holiday from a travel company for you and your family and the holiday 'goes wrong'. You can sue the travel company because you are one of the parties to the contract, but can the members of your family sue the travel company? Are they parties (privy) to the contract?

This chapter will also examine the other side of the principle of privity of contract, that is that a third party cannot have liabilities imposed upon him by a contract to which he has not agreed.

Finally, this chapter will explore the statutory provisions found in the Contracts (Rights of Third Parties) Act 1999 by which a third party can acquire the power to enforce rights under a contract to which he is not a party.

NB Privity of contract is really no more than a 'branch' of 'consideration'.

What we looked at under consideration was that if both parties do not furnish consideration (give each other something) the contract is said to lack consideration and therefore there is no contract.

Under the privity doctrine we are looking at the position of the third party.

If that third party, say Kate, agrees with say Eric and Fred, AND provides consideration then she will be a party to the contract. This means that she can enforce the contract against Eric and Fred. It also means that Eric and Fred can enforce the contract against Kate provided, of course, that they have both provided consideration.

8.2 Common law rule

Only the parties to a contract can be bound by it, or entitled under it.

However, this is now subject to the Contracts (Rights of Third Parties) Act 1999, which is dealt with later.

For example, at common law if A and B make a contract whereby they agree to do something for C, and C is not a party to the contract he cannot enforce it against A or B. Nor can A or B enforce it against C.

In *Tweedle v Atkinson* (1861–73)

>**Wrightman J** said:
>. . . it is now well established that at law no stranger to the consideration can take advantage of the contract though made for his benefit.

8.2.1 Privity example 1

Fred and Eric both agree to give Belinda £100.

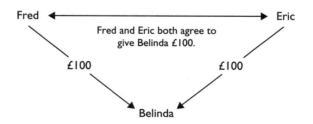

Question: Is there an agreement between Fred and Eric?

The answer is 'Yes'; there is an agreement between Fred and Eric.

The question was whether there was an AGREEMENT – NOT whether there was a CONTRACT.

The facts show that there was an agreement between Fred and Eric.

Question: Have both Fred and Eric provided consideration?

The answer is 'Yes'; both Fred and Eric provided consideration.

Question: Has Eric received a benefit?

'No' is the correct answer.

The question was 'Has Eric RECEIVED a benefit?'.

What did Eric get from the deal? He gets no money or even a promise of some money. So Eric RECEIVES NO benefit from the agreement.

Question: Has Eric suffered a detriment?

'Yes' is the correct answer.

Eric's detriment is the promise to part with his £100.

Question: Has Fred suffered a detriment?

'Yes' is the correct answer.

Fred's detriment is the promise to part with his £100.

Question: Is there a contract between Fred, Eric and Belinda?

'No' is the correct answer.

There might well be an AGREEMENT between the three of them, but there is no contract between the three of them.

Question: Why is there no contract between Fred, Eric and Belinda?

(1) Because although both Eric and Fred suffered a detriment neither party received £100.

(2) Because only Belinda received any money.

(3) Because Belinda furnished no consideration.

The correct answer is '3'.

(1) is incorrect because there is no requirement that a party to a contract must receive a benefit. The test is does one party receive a benefit from the other OR does the other party suffer a detriment.

(2) is irrelevant; it is only there to distract you.

(3) is correct. Belinda has not furnished consideration since she has provided neither Fred nor Eric with a benefit nor has she suffered a detriment at the request of either Fred or Eric.

8.3 The imposition of contractual liabilities upon third parties

The Contracts (Rights of Third Parties) Act 1999 (see later) has not altered this part of the law.

The rule is that two persons cannot, by any contract into which they have entered, **impose liabilities** upon a third party.

8.4 *McGruther v Pitcher* (1904)

McGruther was the owner of a patented 'revolving heel pad'. McGruther pasted inside the lid of each box, in which the pads were sold, a printed slip stating that it was a condition of the sale that they were not to be resold at less than the recommended price, and that 'acceptance of the goods by any purchaser will be deemed to be an acknowledgement that they are sold to him on these conditions and that he agrees with the vendors to be bound by the same'. Pitcher purchased some of the pads from a wholesale agent of McGruther. He then sold them at less than the recommended price. McGruther brought an action against Pitcher to restrain him from selling the pads below the recommended price.

Question: Which of the following is correct?

(1) McGruther could restrain Pitcher from selling the pads below the recommended price because of the contract between the two of them.
(2) McGruther could restrain Pitcher from selling the pads below the recommended price because of the contract between Pitcher and the wholesale agent of McGruther.
(3) McGruther could not restrain Pitcher from selling the pads below the recommended price because there was no contract between the two of them.
(4) McGruther could not restrain Pitcher from selling the pads below the recommended price because although there was a contract between Pitcher and the wholesale agent of McGruther, McGruther himself was not a party to the contract.

A. 1 only   B. 2 only   C. 3 only   D. 4 only   E. 1 & 2   F. 3 & 4

'F' is the correct answer.

(1) is incorrect because there is no contract between McGruther and Pitcher. There is no agreement between them and even if there was McGruther had not provided Pitcher with any consideration. In other words, the privity of contract rule applies.

(2) is incorrect. Even if there was a contract between Pitcher and the whole-sale agent of McGruther, McGruther himself would not be a party to the contract because of the privity of contract rule.

(3) and (4) are correct because there is no contract between McGruther and Pitcher. Since there is no contract between the two of them McGruther cannot claim that Pitcher was in breach of any contract with him by selling the heel pads below the recommended price.

Romer LJ held that the action failed because McGruther could not show that any contract existed between themselves and Pitcher. He said:

> A vendor cannot in that way enforce a condition on the sale of his goods out and out, and, by printing the so-called condition upon some part of goods or on the case containing them, say that every subsequent purchaser of the goods is bound to comply with the condition, so that if he does not comply with the condition he can be sued by the original vendor. That is clearly wrong. You cannot in that way make conditions run with the goods.

8.5 Contracts (Rights of Third Parties) Act 1999

This Act, which came into force on 11 November 1999, was introduced to overcome a long-standing problem in the English law, namely that a third party, that is, someone who was not a party to the contract, could not enforce the contract even if the contract was made specifically for his benefit.

The reason a third party could not enforce such a contract was because he had not furnished consideration to either of the other parties.

The Act now removes this problem.

8.5.1 Right of third party to enforce contractual term – s 1(1)(a)

Section 1(1)(a) of the Contracts (Rights of Third Parties) Act 1999 states:

> ... a person who is not a party to a contract (a 'third party') may in his own right enforce a term of the contract if the contract expressly provides that he may.

Let's reconsider an old favourite.

Fred and Eric both agree to give Belinda £100.

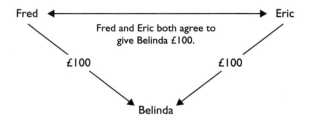

Question: Can Belinda force Eric under s 1(1)(a) to pay her his £100 if he refuses to do so?

(1) Yes   (2) No   (3) Probably

'No' is the correct answer.

Belinda could only force Eric to pay her if the contract between Eric and Fred EXPRESSLY 'provided that she could'.

8.5.2 Right of third party to enforce contractual term – s 1(1)(b)

Section 1(1)(b) of the Contracts (Rights of Third Parties) Act 1999 states:

> . . . a person who is not a party to a contract (a 'third party') may in his own right enforce a term of the contract if the term purports to confer a benefit on him.

Difficulties are likely to arise when the third party tries to rely on a term 'purporting to confer benefits on him'. Section 1(2) provides that s 1(1)(b):

> . . . does not apply if on a proper construction of the contract it appears that the parties did not intend the term to be enforceable by the third party.

For example, Tallis and Deepa may enter into a contract whereby they both agree to give a certain charity £200. This is clearly a contract which purports to confer a benefit on the charity. Since the contract has not expressly stated that the charity may enforce the contract can the charity sue Deepa if she fails to pay them £200? The contract clearly purports to confer a benefit on the charity, BUT did the parties INTEND the term to be enforceable by the charity?

Draughtsmen should be wary of this point when they draft contracts. They should include an express term in the contract giving the third party the right to enforce terms which confer benefits on the third party. For example, in the contract between Tallis and Deepa a clause should be inserted in the contract which states that the charity can sue a party to the contract if they fail to pay the charity £200.

We've seen that s 1(1)(b) of the Contracts (Rights of Third Parties) Act 1999 states:

> ... a person who is not a party to a contract (a 'third party') may in his own right enforce a term of the contract if the term purports to confer a benefit on him.

Let's reconsider our old favourite.

Fred and Eric both agree to give Belinda £100.

Question: Can Belinda force Eric under s 1(1)(b) to pay her his £100 if he refuses to do so?

(1) Yes   (2) No   (3) Probably

'Probably' is the 'best' answer.

The problem with s 1(1)(b) is that it is subject to s 1(2), which provides that s 1(1)(b):

> ... does not apply if on a proper construction of the contract it appears that the parties DID NOT INTEND the term to be enforceable by the third party.

Did Eric and Fred INTEND that Belinda could enforce the contract against them?

Applying the 'objective' test – the rule in *Smith v Hughes* – we might well conclude that Eric and Fred DID INTEND that Belinda could enforce the contract against them.

8.6 Preventing accidental third-party rights under the Act

In order to prevent third parties obtaining enforceable rights 'by accident', a clause should be inserted into the contract which states:

> ... unless expressly provided in this contract, none of the terms or conditions of this contract shall be enforceable by any person who is not a party to the contract.

8.7 Power of the parties to the contract to vary or rescind contract under the Act

Section 2 provides that:

> . . . where a third party has a right to enforce a term of the contract, the parties to the contract may not, by agreement, rescind the contract, or vary it in such a way as to extinguish or alter his entitlement under that right, without his consent.

However, by s 2(3)(a) the parties to the contract may include an express term in their contract which permits them to rescind or vary the contract without the consent of the third party.

For example, Fred and Eric both agree to give Belinda £100 AND they agree that she can enforce their promises to pay her the £100, BUT they include an express term in their contract that they can vary their contract so as to exclude her right to enforce their promises, THEN if they change their minds and say she can't enforce their promises, Belinda will not be able to sue them for their £100s.

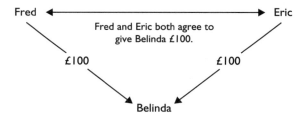

8.8 Contracts excluded from the application of the Act

Section 6 lays down the types of contracts which are excluded, wholly or partly, from the application of the Act. In other words third parties cannot obtain enforceable rights in certain categories of contract.

Such excluded categories include certain employment contracts.

8.9 Contracts for the sale of goods

If now a consumer purchases goods as a gift for a third party, for example, a relative, provided that relative is named or identified (see s 1(3)) AND the seller agrees to it (see s 1(1)(a)), the relative will be able to enforce the seller's obligations that arise under s 14 of the Sale of Goods Act 1979 (goods to of satisfactory quality and fit for purpose) directly against the seller.

If, of course, the relative is not identified or the seller does not agree to the relative obtaining enforceable rights against him, then the relative will have no recourse directly against the seller.

8.10 Travel contracts

If, before the Act, a mother entered into a 'flights only' travel contract on behalf of herself, her husband and her two children then only the mother, strictly speaking, could sue the travel company if the holiday went wrong through the fault of the travel company.

However, if the holiday was a 'package' holiday then the organiser or retailer of the package holiday would be liable to the mother and her family under the Package Travel, Package Holidays and Package Tours Regulations 1992 for the proper performance of the obligations under the contract.

Now, if a mother enters into a 'flights only' travel contract on behalf of herself, her husband and her two children, they are named (see s 1(3)) AND the travel company agrees to it (see s 1(1)(a)), then the whole of the family will be able to enforce the travel contract against the travel company.

8.11 Summary

In this section you've seen:

- that only the parties to a contract can be bound by it, or entitled under it.
- that the privity of contract 'rule' states that no one but the parties to a contract can be bound by it, or entitled under it.
- that two persons cannot, by any contract into which they have entered, impose liabilities upon a third party: see *McGruther v Pitcher* (1904).
- that at common law a third party cannot acquire rights under a contract unless he has provided consideration: see *Tweedle v Atkinson* (1861–73).
- that by using the Contracts (Rights of Third Parties) Act 1999, a third party can acquire the power to enforce rights under a contract to which he is not a party.
- that under the Contracts (Rights of Third Parties) Act 1999 where a third party has a right to enforce a term of the contract, the parties to the contract may not, by agreement, rescind the contract, or vary it in such a way as to extinguish or alter his entitlement under that right, without his consent.

Chapter 9

Terms of the contract

CONTENTS

9.1 Introduction

We have now reached the point where we know that a contract has been validly formed. In this section we will examine the contents of the contract (normally the terms that the parties have agreed to when they formed their contract). We'll be looking at the terms contained in the contract. Traditionally these terms have been divided into conditions (the more important terms) and warranties (the less important terms). However, we'll see that sometimes the terms are not pre-classified into conditions and warranties, but are left in a 'limbo' and classified as innominate terms. It is only when one of the parties to the contract breaks an innominate term that its importance will be considered, this is, should it in the circumstances be now classified as a condition or a warranty?

This section will also examine terms that are implied into a contract. In some cases the terms of a contract will not only consist of the actual terms agreed between the parties to the contract, but sometimes the 'law' will add (imply) extra terms into the contract.

However, to start with, we need to consider what the parties said to each other prior to making the contract. The issue here is whether statements that were made prior to making the contract were intended to be part of the contract. The real difficulty here is that if there is a written contract and the statement that was made prior to that does not appear in the contract can it be claimed that the parties actually intended it to be a term of the contract? If the parties did so intend why then does that term not appear in the written contract?

9.2 Terms and representations

Contract law distinguishes between **terms** and **representations**.

A **term** is **part of a contract**; a **representation** is **NOT part of a contract**.

If a **term** of a contract is **broken** the innocent party can **sue** the contract breaker for **breach of contract**.

If a **representation** turns out not to be true **there can be no breach of contract**, but there may be a possible action for **misrepresentation**; misrepresentation is dealt with later.

In *Behn v Burness* (1863), **Williams J** said:

> Properly speaking, a representation is a statement, or assertion, made by one party to the other, before or at the time of the contract, of some matter or circumstance relating to it. Though it is sometimes contained in the written instrument, it is not an integral part of the contract; and, consequently the contract is not broken though the representation proves to be untrue.

What the above quotation shows is that **not everything** that is said **before**, or **at the time of making the contract**, is **intended** to form part of the actual contract.

In practice it can frequently be very **difficult to distinguish terms from representations**.

9.2.1 Tests to distinguish between terms and representations

The following are points to be considered when trying to distinguish between terms and representations. No one point in itself is conclusive one way or another. In the end a balancing act of the various points has to be attempted.

9.2.2 Time between the making of the statement and the parties entering into the contract

The time between the making of the statement and the parties entering into the contract is one of the factors the court will take into account when determining whether a statement made before the contract was intended to be a mere representation or a term of the contract. Generally speaking, the longer the interval the less likely it will be that the court will hold it was intended to be a term.

Routledge v McKay (1954)

On 23 October the seller of a motor cycle combination told the buyer that it was a late 1941 or 1942 model. The registration book showed it to be first registered on 9 September 1941. The seller in fact knew that the model was a 1936 or 1938 model. A week later on 30 October the seller and buyer entered into a written contract drawn up by the buyer which did not refer to the date of the motor cycle combination. The buyer later discovered the true age of the motor cycle combination and sued the seller for breach of warranty.

> **Sir Raymond Evershed MR** said:
> The question is whether or not, on a sale of a motor bicycle with a side-car combination, there was a warranty as to the date when the machine was originally put on the market . . .
> The [buyer] had caused to be prepared a written memorandum or contract which was signed by himself and the fifth party on Oct. 30, 1949 . . . This written memorandum represents prima facie the record of what the parties intended to agree when the actual transaction took place. Counsel for the [seller] contended that the terms of it necessarily exclude any warranty, that is to say, any collateral bargain, either contemporary or earlier in date . . . [I] think that as a matter of construction it would be difficult to say that such an agreement was consistent with a warranty being given at the same time so as to be intended to form a part of the bargain then made. I think . . . that the last words 'It is understood that when the £30 is paid . . . this transaction is closed' would make such a contention difficult . . .
> . . . in answering the question posed about the date of the motor cycle combination there was anything more intended than a mere representation.

Birch v Paramount Estates (Liverpool) Ltd (1956)

Birch alleged that by an oral warranty he was induced to purchase for £1,825 a house to be built by Paramount Estates. He claimed that he was told his house would be of the same standard of workmanship as the company's show house. In fact the paintwork of his house was inferior to that in the show house and deteriorated faster. Paramount Estates denied any warranty.

The issue before the court was whether Paramount Estates had given a collateral warranty to Birch which became contractually binding when Birch agreed to buy the house.

> **Denning LJ**
> In 1954 Mr. Birch visited a show house on the estate in question and

then went to an incomplete house which he thought he might like to buy. A representative of the builders told him that the house would be just as good as the show house and would be built of materials of the same standard. On July 2, 1954, he signed a contract, a clause in which stated that the house would be built fit for occupation and habitation. The house was, however, very badly painted, much worse than the show house: and the builders had refused to repaint it. [Counsel for the builder] had argued that there was no oral contract and that everything was in the written contract. He had suggested the paintwork was completed by the date of the contract and that, however bad it was, Mr. Birch could not complain. The judgment of the learned County Court judge was however unassailable. It did not matter whether the house was completed on July 2 or not. The oral contract was collateral with the written contract and the builders were liable.

NB In Birch's case there would have been a considerable period between Mr Birch viewing the show house and signing the contract to buy a house, yet the Court of Appeal did not even comment on this point.

9.2.3 Importance on minds of parties

Sometimes the court will consider that a statement that is made is so important to the person to whom it is made, so fundamental to them, that if that statement had not been made to them then they would not have entered into the contract.

Bannerman v White (1861)

During the course of negotiations for the sale of hops by sample White asked Bannerman if any sulphur had been used in the growth or treatment of them, adding that he would not ask the price if sulphur had been used. Bannerman said that no sulphur had been used. After the hops had been delivered White discovered that sulphur had been used in the cultivation of a portion of the hops (5 acres out of 300). However, because the hops were so mixed up together, it was impossible to separate the sulphured from the unsulphured hops. White, therefore, rejected all the hops.

The issue before the court was whether the statement relating to the use of sulphur on the crops was intended to be a mere representation or term of the contract.

Erle CJ

Thus, the question was, – 'Was the affirmation that no sulphur had been used intended between the parties to be part of the contract of sale, and a warranty by the plaintiff?'

. . . the effect is that the defendants required, and that the plaintiff gave his understanding, that no sulphur had been used. This undertaking was a preliminary stipulation; and if it had not been given, the defendants would not have gone on with the treaty which resulted in the sale. In this sense it was the condition upon which the defendants contracted; and it would be contrary to the intention expressed by this stipulation that the contract should remain valid if sulphur had been used.

The intention of the parties governs in the making and in the construction of all contracts. If the parties so intend, the sale may be absolute, with a warranty superadded; or the sale may be conditional, to be null if the warranty is broken. And, upon this statement of facts, we think that the intention appears that the contract should be null if sulphur had been used: and upon this ground we agree that the rule should be discharged.

9.2.4 Later written document

Generally, if, after a statement is made, the contract is put into writing and the representation does not appear in the written contract, the conclusion will be that the parties did not intend the representation to be a term of the contract: if they had intended the representation to be a term of the contract surely they would have put it into the written contract?

See *Routledge v McKay* (above).

9.2.5 One party an expert

If the person making the statement is 'an expert' or in a position to know the true state of affairs then the courts will tend to consider that that statement is intended to have contractual force.

Harling v Eddy (1951)

Sir Raymond Evershed MR
The defendant . . . was offering for sale by auction a large number of Guernsey heifer cows. The catalogue describes them as tuberculin-tested Guernseys, and there is contained in the catalogue a number of conditions, including:

'. . . (12) No animal, article, or thing is sold with a "warranty" unless specially mentioned at the time of offering, and no warranty so given shall have any legal force of effect unless the terms thereof appear on the purchaser's account.'

It appears from the findings of the judge that when this animal No. 9 came into the ring to be sold it received a somewhat frigid reception owing to its unpromising appearance. No one made any bid or evinced any desire to do so. Thereupon the defendant, the seller, who was present, made certain statements . . . The plaintiff said that the defendant stated that there was nothing wrong with the heifer, that he would absolutely guarantee her in every respect, and that he would be willing to take her back if she turned out not to be what he stated she was . . . On this vital matter it is plain that the judge . . . accepted the evidence of the plaintiff . . . defendant having given that description of his animal, the bidding was begun, and in the result the animal was knocked down to the plaintiff for £65.

. . . This animal died in October, and as the result of a post-mortem examination the cause of her death was found to be tuberculosis . . .

The question is: Does the statement which the defendant made at the sale immediately before the bidding entitle the plaintiff now to say: 'The animal was not as you stated her to be, sound in every respect, and I now take advantage of the offer you made to me and claim from you the price I paid for the animal, or equivalent damages'? The difficulty arises from the circumstance that No. 12 of the conditions, which I have already read, prima facie seems intended to render nugatory any mere warranty given at the sale . . .

. . . Does No. 12 of the conditions apply? In my judgment, the answer is: No. Condition No. 12 is limited in its terms to a statement made which is a mere warranty and is not a condition, and the language in the second part of it, '. . . and no warranty so given shall have any legal force or effect . . .' can only refer to the warranty previously mentioned, viz., a statement which is a warranty and no more. In other words, in my judgment, condition No. 12 cannot be relied on by the defendant to defeat the right of the plaintiff to sue for damages for the breach of the condition under which he purchased.

9.2.6 Above tests not conclusive

The above tests are not conclusive in themselves. The main test is that of contractual intention.

In *Heilbut, Symons & Co v Buckleton* (1913), **Lord Moulton** said:

> . . . The intention of the parties can only be deduced from the totality of the evidence, and no secondary principles of such a kind can be universally true.

9.3 Express terms

Express terms are the terms **expressly (actually) agreed** between the parties, for example, the sale of a specific car for £1,000.

Remember that the express terms of the contract are those **agreed** between the parties. It is up to the parties to agree **whichever terms they wish**.

'Contract Law' lays down very few restrictions on what parties may legally agree.

9.3.1 Conditions and warranties

Traditionally, all express terms in a contract were classified as either a **condition or** a **warranty**. This was important when it came to **breach** of a contract term by one of the parties to the contract.

If the term that was broken was a **condition** then the innocent party could, if they wished, **accept** the breach and the contract as **ended**; they could **also sue for damages**.

If the term that was broken was a **warranty** then the innocent party could **only sue for damages**; the contract **continued in existence**.

In practice it can be difficult to lay down a test so as to distinguish between conditions and warranties.

9.3.2 Should every term in a contract be labelled a condition?

These days if a contract specifically states that a certain term is a **condition** does it automatically follow that it is a condition?

Schuler AG v Wickman Machine Tool Sales Ltd (1973)
Schuler granted Wickman the sole right to sell Schuler's products in the UK.

Clause 7 of their agreement provided:

> (a) [Wickman] will use its best endeavours to promote and extend the sale of Schuler products in the [UK]. (b) It shall be condition of this Agreement that (i) [Wickman] shall send its representative to visit the six firms whose names are listed in the Schedule hereto at least once in every week for the purpose of soliciting orders for panel presses; (ii) that the same representative shall visit each firm on each occasion unless there are unavoidable reasons preventing the visit being made by that representative.

Clause 11 provided that the agreement could be determined forthwith if:

> (i) the other shall have committed a material breach of its obligations hereunder and shall have failed to remedy the same within 60 days of being required in writing so to do.

Wickman failed to make all the necessary visits required by clause 7(b). Schuler claimed that since Wickman had broken their obligations under clause 7, which was a condition of the contract, that breach of the condition entitled them to treat Wickman's breach as bringing the contract to an end.

The issue before the court was whether clause 7 was a condition of the contract.

The court **held** that looking at the true INTENTION of the parties they had not INTENDED Clause 7 to be a condition DESPITE the fact that they had DESCRIBED it as a condition in their contract.

NB *Schuler AG v Wickman Machine Tool Sales Ltd* illustrates the point that in many contract cases **there is no issue about one party having broken the contract**; the contract breaker very often admits his breach of contract.

In the **Schuler case** Wickman **admitted** their breach.

In that case the dispute was about a **term of the contract**. In many cases the dispute is as to the size of the damages that can be claimed.

9.4 'Modern' approach to classifying terms

9.4.1 Innominate terms

The modern 'academic' approach is not to pre-classify terms at all, but to 'wait and see' how serious the effect of the breach of contract is.

If the effect of the breach is serious, the term is a condition.

If the effect of the breach is not very serious, the term is a warranty.

This was the approach developed in the *Hong Kong Fir Shipping* case (1962).

However, it is still possible to pre-classify terms as conditions and this is the approach still taken by contract draughtsmen.

The Mihalis Angelos (1970)

The owners of the vessel *Mihalis Angelos* chartered it to the charterers for a voyage from Haiphong to Hamburg. In the charterparty the owners stated that the vessel was 'expected ready to load under this charter about 1 July 1965': they had no reasonable grounds in saying that she was 'expected to load' on that date.

The issue before the court was whether the 'readiness' clause was a condition of the contract.

This time the court held that the 'readiness' clause was a condition of the contract!

You probably have thought that following *Schuler AG v Wickman Machine Tool Sales Ltd* the 'readiness' clause was a warranty, but the court thought differently.

> **Megaw LJ** said:
> In my judgement, such a term in a charterparty ought to be regarded as being a condition of the contract, in the old sense of the word 'condition', ie that when it has been broken, the other party can, if he wishes, by

intimation to the party in breach, elect to be released from performance of his further obligations under the contract . . .

I reach that conclusion . . . it tends towards certainty in the law. One of the essential elements of law is some measure of uniformity. One of the important elements of the law is predictability. At any rate in commercial law, there are obvious and substantial advantages in having, where possible, a firm and definite rule for a particular class of legal relationship, eg as here, the legal categorisation of a particular, definable type of contractual clause in common use. It is surely much better, both for shipowners and charterers (and, incidentally, for their advisers) when a contractual obligation of this nature is under consideration, and still more when they are faced with the necessity for an urgent decision as to the effects of a suspected breach of it, to be able to say categorically: 'If a breach is proved, then the charterer can put an end to the contract', rather than that they should be left to ponder whether or not the courts would be likely, in the particular case, when the evidence had been heard, to decide that in the particular circumstances the breach was or was not such as to go to the root of the contract. Where justice does not require greater flexibility, there is everything to be said for, and nothing against, a degree of rigidity in legal principle.

9.5 Implied terms

In addition to the terms **expressly** agreed between the parties there are sometimes terms **implied** into the contract. In such cases, therefore, in order to determine what the exact contract (agreement) is between the parties the **express terms AND the implied terms** must be taken **together**: together they constitute the **one** contract between the parties.

NB Terms can be implied into a contract by custom, statute or by the court.

9.5.1 Terms implied by custom

In many 'trades' or areas of business there are to be found customs of various sorts. These customs can include 'legal' customs which have the effect of implying terms into a contract. To imply a term into such a contract the custom must be 'notorious, certain, legal and reasonable'.

In *Hutton v Warren* (1836), **Parke B** said:

It has long been settled, that, in commercial transactions, extrinsic evidence of custom and usage is admissible to annex incidents to written contracts, in matters with respect to which they are silent. The same rule has also been applied to contracts in other transactions of life, in which known usages have been established and prevailed; and this has been done upon the principle of presumption that, in such transactions, the parties did not mean to express in writing the whole of the contract by which they intended to be bound, but a contract with reference to those known usages.

NB Such a term will only be implied into a contract where there is nothing in the written contract which expressly or impliedly excludes the customary term.

Lynch v Thorne (1956)

Under a written contract a builder agreed to sell to the buyer a house which was still being built. The builder covenanted to complete the building in accordance with a plan and specification attached to the agreement. Within two weeks of the buyer moving into the house rain came in through some of the windows and a damp patch appeared in the south wall of a room on the first floor. The buyer alleged that it was an implied term of the contract that the house should be completed in a workmanlike manner, with proper materials, and should, when completed, be reasonably fit for human habitation.

The issue before the court was whether a term could be implied into a contract so as to contradict an express term of that contract.

Lord Evershed MR

... I am, however, prepared to assume for the purposes of this judgment that, whether or not it can be said that any necessity so compels in the case where a vendor contracts to sell the land and also to complete the building, in such a case prima facie there is an implied covenant on the vendor builder's part that he will complete the house so as to make it habitable. Nevertheless, although such a term is prima facie to be implied, it must, according to well-established principle, always yield to the express letter of the bargain ...

No one has sought to quarrel with the learned judge's findings of fact, and, so far as I can see, no one could quarrel with them. The judge, after referring to the plan and to the specification, said: 'It is not disputed that the house has been built exactly in accordance with the drawings and specification.' ...

The effect of ... those findings seems to me to be that, the contract having provided that the house should be built and completed in a particular way by the use of particular materials of particular characteristics, the defendant precisely and exactly complied with his obligation. He is also found to have shown, through his servants, a high standard of workmanship ...

... I can find no room for an implied warranty, the only effect of the operation of which would, so far as I can see, be to create an inconsistency with the express language of the bargain made.

9.5.2 Terms implied by statute

Examples of terms implied into contracts by statute are to be found in the Sale of Goods Act 1979.

For example, the **Sale of Goods Act 1979 s 14(2)** provides that:

> Where the seller sells goods in the course of a business, there is an implied term that the goods supplied under the contract are of **satisfactory quality**.

Similarly, s 14(3) implies a term into contracts of sale that goods are **fit for the purpose**. Section 14(3) provides that:

> Where the seller sells goods in the course of a business and the buyer, expressly or by implication, makes known – (a) to the seller . . . any particular purpose for which the goods are being bought, there is an implied term that the goods supplied under the contract are reasonably fit for that purpose . . .

9.5.3 Terms implied by the courts

In **very exceptional** circumstances the court **may** (doesn't have to) be prepared to imply a term into a contract.

NB As a general rule the courts are **most reluctant** to imply terms into any contract.

9.5.3.1 'The Moorcock' principle

The courts will imply a term to give 'business efficacy' to the contract (the so-called '**The Moorcock**' principle). This is on the basis of the 'presumed intention' of the parties. **Remember** that the courts are **most reluctant** to imply a term into a contract and they will only imply a term into a contract on *The Moorcock* principle where the contract would otherwise fail.

This principle **should never be relied upon**! The motto is '**draft the contract correctly in the first place**'.

The Moorcock (1887)

The appellant wharfingers owned a wharf and a jetty which extended into the River Thames. The respondent was the owner of the steamship *Moorcock*. In November 1887 it was agreed between the appellants and the respondent that the *Moorcock* should be discharged and loaded at the wharf and for that purpose should be moored alongside the jetty where she would take the ground at low water. No charge was made in respect of the vessel being moored alongside the jetty, but the shipowner paid for the use of the cranes in discharging the cargo, and rates were payable to the appellants on all goods

landed, shipped or stored. Whilst the *Moorcock* was lying moored at the end
of the jetty discharging her cargo, the tide ebbed and she grounded with the
result that she sustained damage owing to the centre of the vessel settling on a
ridge of hard ground beneath the mud.

The issue before the court was whether there should be implied into the
contract a term that the wharfinger had taken reasonable care to ascertain
that the bottom of the river at the jetty was in such a condition as not to
endanger the vessel.

Bowen LJ

... The question which arises in this case is whether, when a contract
is made to let the use of this jetty to a ship which can only use it, as is
known by both parties, by her taking the ground, there is any implied
warranty on the part of the wharfingers [owners], and if so what is the
extent of the warranty.

What did each party in the present case know because, if we are examining into their presumed intention, we must examine into their minds as
to what the transaction was. Both parties knew that this jetty was let for
the purpose of profit, and knew that it could only be used by the ship
taking the ground and lying on the ground. They must have known that it
was by grounding that she would use the jetty. They must have known,
both of them, that unless the ground was safe the ship would be simply
buying an opportunity of danger and buying no convenience at all, and
that all consideration would fail unless the ground was safe. In fact,
the business of the jetty could not be carried on unless, I do not say the
ground was safe, it was supposed to be safe. The master and crew of the
ship could know nothing, whereas the defendants or their servants might,
by exercising reasonable care, know everything. The defendants or their
servants were on the spot at high and low tide, morning and evening.
They must know what had happened to the ships that had used the jetty
before, and with the slightest trouble they could satisfy themselves in case
of doubt whether the berth was or not safe. The ship's officers, on the
other hand, had no means of verifying the state of the berth, because,
for aught I know, it might be occupied by another ship at the time the
Moorcock got there.

... it may well be said that the law will not imply that the defendants,
who had not control of the place, ought to have taken reasonable care to
make the berth good, but it does not follow that they are relieved from all
responsibility, a responsibility which depends not merely on the control
of the place, which is one element as to which the law implies a duty, but
on other circumstances. The defendants are on the spot. They must know
the jetty cannot be safely used unless reasonable care is taken. No one
can tell whether reasonable safety has been secured except themselves,
and I think that, if they let out their jetty for use, they at all events imply

that they have taken reasonable care to see that the berth, which is the essential part of the use of the jetty, is safe, and, if it is not safe, and if they have not taken such reasonable care, it is their duty to warn persons with whom they have dealings that they have not done so . . .

9.5.3.2 Term implied as a legal incident of particular kind of contract

Here the court is not trying to imply a term into a **concluded** contract, but rather it is trying to establish what the **full** contract is.

Liverpool CC v Irwin (1976)

The Irwins were tenants of a flat owned by Liverpool City Council. The tenancy agreement imposed many obligations on the tenants, but none on the landlord, Liverpool City Council. The tenants complained of continual failure of the lifts, lack of lighting on the stairs, dangerous condition of the staircase and frequent blockage of the rubbish chutes. Eventually the tenants considered that they had suffered enough problems and refused to pay their rent. In response to this the landlords sought an order for possession of the tenants' flats. The tenants counterclaimed alleging that the landlord was in breach of an implied term to keep the common parts of the flats in repair and properly lighted.

The issue before the court was whether a term could be implied into the tenancy agreement and, if so, on what basis.

Lord Wilberforce
. . . The court here is simply concerned to establish what the contract is, the parties not having themselves fully stated the terms. In this sense the court is searching for what must be implied.

What then should this contract be held to be? There must first be implied a letting, ie a grant of the right of exclusive possession to the tenants. With this there must, I would suppose, be implied a covenant for quiet enjoyment, as a necessary incident of the letting. The difficulty begins when we consider the common parts. We start with the fact that the demise is useless unless access is obtained by the staircase; we can add that, having regard to the height of the block, and the family nature of the dwellings, the demise would be useless without a lift service; we can continue that there being rubbish chutes built in to the structures and no other means of disposing of light rubbish there must be a right to use the chutes. The question to be answered – and it is the only question in this case – is what is to be the legal relationship between landlord and tenant as regards these matters.

There can be no doubt that there must be implied (i) an easement for the tenants and their licensees to use the stairs, (ii) a right in the nature of an easement to use the lifts and (iii) an easement to use the rubbish chutes.

But are these easements to be accompanied by any obligation on the landlord, and what obligation? There seem to be two alternatives. The first, for which the corporation contends, is for an easement coupled with no legal obligation, except such as may arise under the Occupiers' Liability Act 1957 as regards the safety of those using the facilities, and possibly such other liability as might exist under the ordinary law of tort. The alternative is for easements coupled with some obligation on the part of the landlords as regards the maintenance of the subject of them, so that they are available for use.

My Lords, in order to be able to choose between these, it is necessary to define what test is to be applied, and I do not find this difficult. In my opinion such obligation should be read into the contract as the nature of the contract itself implicitly requires, no more, no less; a test in other words of necessity. The relationship accepted by the corporation is that of landlord and tenant; the tenant accepts obligations accordingly, in relation, inter alia, to the stairs, the lifts and the chutes . . .

It remains to define the standard. My Lords, if, as I think, the test of the existence of the term is necessity the standard must surely not exceed what is necessary having regard to the circumstances. To imply an absolute obligation to repair would go beyond what is a necessary legal incident and would indeed be unreasonable. An obligation to take reasonable care to keep in reasonable repair and usability is what fits the requirements of the case . . .

9.6 Summary

In this section you've seen:

- that contract law distinguishes between terms and representations. A term is part of a contract; a representation is not part of a contract: see *Behn v Burness* (1863).
- that not everything that is said before, or at the time of making the contract, is intended to form part of the actual contract.
- that when trying to distinguish terms from representations you need to consider:
  - the lapse of time between the statement being made and the contract being formed;
  - the importance on anything said on the minds of parties: What importance did both parties attach to the statement?;
  - whether there is a later written document: generally, if after a statement is made the contract is put into writing and the representation does not appear in the written contract the conclusion will be that the parties did not intend the representation to be a term of the contract;

- ○ that a statement may be considered to be a term of the contract because it was made by an expert to a non expert; and
- ○ remember that the above tests are not conclusive: the main test is that of contractual intention.

- that express terms are the terms expressly (actually) agreed between the parties, e.g. the sale of a specific pen for £5.
- that traditionally, all express terms in a contract were classified as either conditions or warranties.
- that if the term that was broken was a condition then the innocent party could, if they wished, accept the breach as a repudiatory breach and thus the contract would be at an end; they could also sue for damages.
- that if the term that was broken was a warranty then the innocent party could only sue for damages; the contract continued in existence.
- that the modern approach to classifying terms is not to pre-classify them at all, but to 'wait and see' how serious the effect of the breach of contract is; they are all innominate terms. If the effect of the breach is serious the term is a condition; if the effect of the breach is not very serious then the term is a warranty: see *The Hong Kong Fir Shipping* case (1962).
- that in addition to the terms expressly agreed between the parties there are sometimes terms implied into the contract. In such cases in order to determine what the exact contract (agreement) is between the parties the express terms AND the implied terms must be taken together: together they constitute the one contract between the parties.
- that terms can be implied by custom, by statute or by the courts.
- that the courts will imply a term to give 'business efficacy' to the contract. This is on the basis of the 'presumed intention' of the parties: see *The Moorcock* (1887).
- that the courts are most reluctant to imply a term into a contract and they will only imply a term into a contract on *The Moorcock* principle where the contract would otherwise fail.
- that *The Moorcock* is a strict test. The test is not only what is a 'reasonable' term by whether it is also a 'necessary' term: see *Liverpool CC v Irwin* (1976).

Chapter 10

Exemption clauses –
the common law

10.1 Introduction

When drafting a contract the parties should consider what will happen if either of them breaks a term of the contract. The consequences of such a breach have already been examined in the chapter on 'Terms of the contract' and will be discussed further below in the chapter on 'Remedies for breach of contract'. This chapter deals with the common law aspects of exemption clauses (exclusion clauses) found in contracts. The purpose of an exemption clause is to exempt, or limit, the liability of a party who breaks a term of the contract. The courts have an inherent dislike of exemption clauses and so have been very strict in the interpretation of such clauses. This chapter examines whether an exemption clause has been incorporated into a contract, whether that exemption clause is actually effective and finally if that exemption clause, although validly incorporated into the contract, has been rendered invalid or inoperative for some reason.

10.2 Exemption clauses

Definition

An exemption (exclusion) clause is one whereby one party to a contract inserts into a contract a term excluding or limiting his potential
liability for any future breach of contract by him.

Although there are now statutory provisions (see the Unfair Contract Terms
Act 1977 below), it is still important to consider the common law relating to
exemption clauses because not all exemption clauses are covered by the
Unfair Contract Terms Act 1977.

10.3 Incorporation of exemption clause into the contract

The exemption clause must be incorporated into the contract – if it is not
then it does not form part of the agreement between the parties and therefore
will not bind them.

10.4 Ways in which exemption clauses can be incorporated into a contract

10.4.1 Is the document intended to have contractual effect?

An exemption clause will not be incorporated into a contract if the document
containing the exemption clause was not intended to have contractual force.

Chapelton v Barry UDC (1940)

Slesser LJ
On June 3, 1939, Mr Chapelton went on to the beach at a place
called Cold Knap, which is within the area of the Barry Urban District
Council, and wished to sit down in a deck chair. On the beach, by the side
of a cafe, was a pile of deck chairs belonging to the defendants, and by
the side of the deck chairs there was a notice put up in these terms: 'Barry
Urban District Council. Cold Knap. Hire of chairs, 2d per session of 3
hours.' Then followed words which said that the public were respectfully
requested to obtain tickets for their chairs from the chair attendants, and
that those tickets must be retained for inspection.
  Mr Chapelton, having taken two chairs from the attendant, one for
himself and one for a Miss Andrews, who was with him, received two
tickets from the attendant, glanced at them, and slipped them into his
pocket. He said in the court below that he had no idea that there were
any conditions on those tickets and that he did not know anything

about what was on the back of them. He took the chairs to the beach and put them up in the ordinary way, setting them up firmly on a flat part of the beach, but when he sat down he had the misfortune to go through the canvas, and, unfortunately, had a bad jar, the result of which was that he suffered injury and had to see a doctor, and in respect of that he brought his action.

Questions of this sort are always questions of difficulty and are very often largely questions of fact. In the class of case where it is said that there is a term in the contract freeing railway companies, or other providers of facilities, from liabilities which they would otherwise incur at common law, it is a question as to how far that condition has been made a term of the contract and whether it has been sufficiently brought to the notice of the person entering into the contract with the railway company, or other body, and there is a large number of authorities on that point. In my view, however, the present case does not come within that category at all. I think that the contract here, as appears from a consideration of all the circumstances, was this: The local authority offered to hire chairs to persons to sit upon on the beach, and there was a pile of chairs there standing ready for use by any one who wished to use them, and the conditions on which they offered persons the use of those chairs were stated in the notice which was put up by the pile of chairs, namely, that the sum charged for the hire of a chair was 2d per session of three hours. I think that was the whole of the offer which the local authority made in this case. They said, in effect: 'We offer to provide you with a chair, and if you accept that offer and sit in the chair, you will have to pay for that privilege 2d per session of three hours.'

. . . I do not think that the notice excluding liability was a term of the contract at all . . .

Burnett v Westminster Bank Ltd (1965)

Burnett had two accounts with Westminster Bank; one was with the Borough branch and the other was with the Bromley branch. He wrote a cheque for £2,300 on a cheque from his Borough branch cheque book, but he crossed out Borough and its address and substituted Bromley and its address. He initialed the alterations. He then decided to stop the cheque. He telephoned the Bromley branch and told them the correct number and date of the cheque and its amount and also that it was a Borough cheque altered to Bromley and instructed them not to pay the cheque. He confirmed these instructions by letter to the Bromley branch. However, the bank did not stop the cheque and his account was debited with £2,300. Burnett claimed £2,300 stating that the bank acted without his authority when they debited his account at the Borough branch. The bank's defence was that it was an express term of contract between themself and Burnett that cheques issued by the Borough branch would be applied only to that account and no other account. The bank claimed that these terms were incorporated into the contract between themself and Burnett from the notice printed on the front cover of the cheque book, which stated that 'the cheques in this book will be applied to the account for which they have been prepared. Customers must not, therefore, permit their use on any other account'. The bank argued that notwithstanding the alterations Burnett had made to the cheque it must be read as a mandate to the Borough branch with which they had complied.

The issue before the court was whether the notice in the cheque book had been incorporated into the contract between the bank and Burnett.

Mocatta J

... The restriction could only be made effective by agreement between the plaintiff and the defendants ... The defendants argued, however, that the plaintiff had, by his conduct in using a cheque or cheques taken from the new cheque book containing on the front of its cover the two sentences which I have set out, agreed to the restriction in question.

... Here the plaintiff and defendants had been in contractual relationship, since the plaintiff first opened his account with the defendants at their Borough branch. If two sentences on the face of the cheque book are to have contractual effect that must be by way of variation of the already existing contract between the parties. The effect of this distinction, however, is in my judgment merely to emphasise the importance of the notice to be given by the defendants to their customer before they can be in a position to plead successfully that he has accepted the proposed variation by using a cheque from the new book.

Despite counsel for the defendants' able argument I am unable to treat the two sentences on the cheque book cover as adequate notice ... But in the case of a customer like the plaintiff who has had an account for some time under the system prevailing down to the issue of the new cheque book, I am of the opinion that the mere presence of the two sentences on the new cheque book cover is inadequate to affect the pre-existing contractual relationship. In such circumstances I do not consider that the defendants could establish that they had given adequate notice to their customer to bind him to the new restricted use of the cheques unless they could show that he had read the sentences in question, or had signed some document indicating his agreement to their effect. I would be prepared to accept as the equivalent of the latter the signature of the customer on a cheque provided that the cheque form itself bore words limiting its use to the bank, branch and account shown in print on it. The present cheque bore no such words.

I accordingly declare that the plaintiff is entitled to have his Borough account with the defendants credited by them with £2,300.

10.4.2 Signing the contract

If the parties to a contract sign it, they will be bound by its terms, including any exclusion clauses contained in the contract.

L'Estrange v Graucob Ltd (1934)

L'Estrange signed a contract to purchase a cigarette vending machine from Graucob. The contract stated:

> This agreement contains all the terms and conditions under which I agree to purchase the machine specified above, and any express or implied condition, statement, or warranty, statutory or otherwise not stated herein is hereby excluded.

The machine turned out to be defective so L'Estrange rejected it claiming that it was not fit for the purpose for which it was sold (term implied into the contract by the Sale of Goods Act 1893). Graucob claimed that the agreement expressly provided for the exclusion of all implied warranties. L'Estrange said although she did not read the agreement she did sign it intentionally.

The issue before the court was whether the exclusion clause formed part of the contract.

The court held that the clause did form part of the contract. The court said:

> L'Estrange having put her signature to the contract cannot be heard to say that she is not bound by the terms of the document because she has not read them.

Scrutton LJ

The main question raised in the present case is whether that clause formed part of the contract. If it did, it clearly excluded any condition or warranty.

(1): 'In an ordinary case, where an action is brought on a written agreement which is signed by the defendant, the agreement is proved by proving his signature, and, in the absence of fraud, it is wholly immaterial that he has not read the agreement and does not know its contents.'

When a document containing contractual terms is signed, then, in the absence of fraud, or, I will add, misrepresentation, the party signing it is bound, and it is wholly immaterial whether he has read the document or not . . .

In this case the plaintiff has signed a document headed 'Sales Agreement', which she admits had to do with an intended purchase, and which contained a clause excluding all conditions and warranties. That being so, the plaintiff, having put her signature to the document and not having been induced to do so by any fraud or misrepresentation, cannot be heard to say that she is not bound by the terms of the document because she has not read them.

10.4.3 Incorporation by reasonable notice

An exemption clause will be incorporated into a contract if the party seeking to rely on it gives reasonable notice that the document contains conditions. The test is whether reasonable notice has been given of the exemption clause.

Parker v South Eastern Railway Co (1877)

Parker had deposited his bag in the cloakroom at the defendant's railway station. He paid the clerk 2d and was given a ticket which on the face of it said 'See back.' On the other side were several clauses one of which said 'The company will not be responsible for any package exceeding the value of £10'. On returning to the cloakroom Parker presented his ticket to the clerk but the bag could not be found. Parker claimed £24 10s as the value of his bag. The company pleaded that Parker had accepted the goods on the condition that they would not be responsible for the value if it exceeded £10. At the trial, **Pollock B** asked the jury: (1) Did Parker read, or was he aware of, the special condition upon which the articles were deposited? (2) Was he, in the circumstances, under any obligation, in the exercise of reasonable and proper caution, to read or make himself aware of the condition? The jury answered both questions in the negative and judgment was given for Parker.

On appeal the issue before the court was whether the clause on the back of the ticket had been incorporated into the contract between Parker and the railway company.

Mellish LJ

. . . The question then is, whether the plaintiff was bound by the conditions contained in the ticket? . . . Now if in the course of making a contract one party delivers to another a paper containing writing, and the party receiving the paper knows that the paper contains conditions which the party delivering it intends to constitute the contract, I have no doubt that the party receiving the paper does, by receiving and keeping it, assent to the conditions contained in it, although he does not read them, and does not know what they are . . .

. . . Now the question we have to consider is whether the railway company were entitled to assume that the person depositing luggage, and receiving a ticket in such a way that he could see that some writing was printed on it, were entitled to assume that the person receiving it would understand that the writing contained the conditions of contract, and this seems to me to depend upon whether people in general would, in fact and naturally, draw that inference. The railway company, as it seems to me, must be entitled to make some assumptions respecting the person who deposits luggage with them. I think they are entitled to assume that he can read, and that he understands the English language, and that he pays such attention to what he is about as may be reasonably expected from a person in such a transaction as that of depositing luggage in a cloakroom. The railway company must, however, take mankind as they find them, and if what they do is sufficient to inform people in general that the ticket contains conditions, I think that a particular plaintiff ought not to be in a better position than other persons on account of his exceptional ignorance or stupidity or carelessness; but if what the railway company do is not sufficient to convey to the minds of people in general that the ticket contains conditions, then they have received goods on deposit without obtaining the consent of the persons depositing them to the conditions limiting their liability.

I am of opinion, therefore, that the proper direction to leave to the jury in these cases is, that if the person receiving the ticket did not see or know that there was any writing on the ticket, he is not bound by the conditions; that if he knew there was writing, and knew or believed that the writing contained conditions, that then he is bound by the conditions, that if he knew there was writing on the ticket, but did not know or believe that the writing contained conditions, nevertheless he would be bound, if the delivering of the ticket to him in such a manner that he could see there was writing upon it, was, in the opinion of the jury, reasonable notice that the writing contained conditions . . .

10.4.3.1 Have reasonable steps been taken to draw the notice to the attention of the other party?

The party seeking to rely on the exemption clause need not show that he has actually brought it to the notice of the other party, but only that he took reasonable steps to do so.

See *Parker v South Eastern Railway Co* (above).

Thompson v London, Midland and Scottish Railway Co (1930)

Aldcroft, Thompson's niece, bought a half day excursion ticket for her aunt who was illiterate. On the face of the ticket were printed the words 'Excursion. For conditions see back', and on the back of the ticket were printed the words 'Issued subject to the conditions and regulations in the company's time tables'. In the company's timetable (which had to be bought for 6d) were printed the words: 'Excursion tickets . . . are issued subject to the general regulations and to the condition that the holders . . . shall have no rights of action against the company . . . in respect of . . . injury (fatal or otherwise) . . . however caused.' Thompson was injured as a result of the alleged negligence of the railway company. The railway company relied on the exemption from liability provisions contained in the timetable.

The issue before the court was whether the railway company had taken reasonable steps to bring the conditions to the notice of Thompson.

Lord Hanworth MR

It appears to me that the right way of considering such notices is put by Swift J in *Nunan v. Southern Ry. Co*. After referring to a number of cases which have been dealt with in the Courts he says: 'I am of opinion that the proper method of considering such a matter is to proceed upon the assumption that where a contract is made by the delivery, by one of the contracting parties to the other, of a document in a common form stating the terms upon which the person delivering it will enter into the proposed contract, such a form constitutes the offer of the party who tenders it, and if the form is accepted without objection by the person to whom it is tendered this person is as a general rule bound by its contents and his act amounts to an acceptance of the offer to him whether he reads the document or otherwise informs himself of its contents or not, and the conditions contained in the document are binding upon him.' In law it seems to me that that is right. The railway company is to be treated as having made an offer to intending travelers that if they will accept the conditions on which the railway company make the offer they can be taken at suitable times, on suitable days and by indicated trains from Darwen to Manchester and back at a price largely reduced from the common price; but upon certain conditions which can be ascertained, and of the existence of which there can be no doubt, for they are indicated clearly upon the ticket which is issued.

. . . it appears to me that when that ticket was taken it was taken with the knowledge that the conditions applied, and that the person who took the ticket was bound by those conditions. If that be so, the conditions render it impossible for the plaintiff to succeed in her action . . .

. . . It is quite clear, therefore, that it was intended there should be a ticket issued; and on that ticket plainly on its face is a reference made to the conditions under which it is issued.

. . . So here the giving of the ticket in plain terms indicated that there are conditions, and that one of the conditions is that the person shall find them at a certain place and accept them, and that is I think quite a plain indication that the carrier has made that offer upon terms and conditions only, and that any answer that he had not brought the conditions sufficiently to the notice of the person accepting the offer must be set aside as perverse.

Thornton v Shoe Lane Parking Ltd (1971)

Thornton drove his car up to the barrier of a multi-storey car park which he had not parked in before. Outside the car park was a notice which said at the bottom 'All Cars Parked At Owners Risk'. Thornton took a parking ticket from the machine at the barrier; on the ticket was printed 'This ticket is issued subject to the conditions of issue as displayed on the premises'. He looked at the ticket to see the time on it. He saw that there was printing on the ticket, but he did not read it. If he had read the ticket he would have had to walk around the car park to search for the conditions. He then drove into the car park. When he returned he paid the car park charge. Whilst putting his belongings into the boot of his car there was an accident and he was severely injured. One of the conditions displayed in the car park said that Shoe Lane Parking 'shall not be responsible . . . for any . . . injury to the Customer . . . occurring when the Customer's motor vehicle is in the Parking Building howsoever that . . . injury shall be caused'. Shoe Lane Parking claimed that this clause exempted them from any liability to Thornton.

The issue before the court was whether the clause was incorporated into the contract.

Lord Denning MR

None of those [ticket] cases has any application to a ticket which is issued by an automatic machine. The customer pays his money and gets a ticket. He cannot refuse it. He cannot get his money back. He may protest to the machine, even swear at it; but it will remain unmoved. He is committed beyond recall. He was committed at the very moment when he put his money into the machine. The contract was concluded at that time. It can be translated into offer and acceptance in this way. The offer is made when the proprietor of the machine holds it out as being ready to receive the money. The acceptance takes place when the customer puts his money into the slot. The terms of the offer are contained in the notice placed on or near the machine stating what is offered for the money. The customer is bound by those terms as long as they are sufficiently brought to his notice beforehand, but not otherwise. He is not bound by the terms printed on the ticket if they differ from the notice, because the ticket comes too late. The contract has already been made: see *Olley v Marlborough Court Ltd*. The ticket is no more than a voucher or receipt for the money that has been paid (as in the deckchair case, *Chapelton v Barry Urban District Council*), on terms which have been offered and accepted before the ticket is issued. In the present case the offer was contained in the notice at the entrance giving the charges for garaging and saying 'at owners risk', ie at the risk of the owner so far as damage to the car was concerned. The offer was accepted when the plaintiff drove up to the entrance and, by the movement of his car, turned the light from red to green, and the ticket was thrust at him. The contract was then concluded, and it could not be altered by any words printed on the ticket itself. In particular, it could not be altered so as to exempt the company from liability for personal injury due to their negligence.

I do not think the defendants can escape liability by reason of the exempting condition. I would, therefore, dismiss the appeal.

10.4.4 Time of notice

Was the exclusion clause brought to the attention of the other party before or after the making of the contract?

Olley v Marlborough Court Ltd (1949)

Olley had reserved a room at the Marlborough Court hotel. On registering at the hotel Olley paid for a week's accommodation in advance. In her bedroom was a notice which stated:

> The proprietors will not hold themselves responsible for articles lost or stolen unless handed to the manageress for safe custody. Valuables should be deposited for safe custody in a sealed package and a receipt obtained.

Whilst out of her room various articles of hers worth £329 were stolen.

Having decided that Marlborough Court was negligent, the issue before the court was whether the exclusion clause had been incorporated into the contract.

Denning LJ

The only other point is whether the defendants are protected by the notice which they put in the plaintiff's bedroom providing:

> 'The proprietors will not hold themselves responsible for articles lost or stolen unless handed to the manageress for safe custody.'

The first question is whether that notice formed part of the contract. People who rely on a contract to exempt themselves from their common law liability must prove that contract strictly. Not only must the terms of the contract be clearly proved, but also the intention to create legal relations – the intention to be legally bound – must also be clearly proved. The best way of proving it is by a written document signed by the party to be bound. Another way is by handing him, before or at the time of the contract, a written notice specifying certain terms and making it clear to him that the contract is in those terms. A prominent public notice which is plain for him to see when he makes the contract would, no doubt, have the same effect, but nothing short of one of these three ways will suffice. It has been held that mere notices put on receipts for money do not make a contract: see *Chapelton v Barry UDC*. So, also, in my opinion, notices put up in bedrooms do not of themselves make a contract. As a rule, the guest does not see them until after he has been accepted as a guest. The hotel company, no doubt, hope that the guest will be held bound by them, but the hope is vain unless they clearly show that he agreed to be bound by them, which is rarely the case.

10.4.5 Reasonableness of notice depends on extent of exclusion

Interfoto Picture Library Ltd v Stiletto Visual Programmes Ltd (1988)
Stiletto telephoned Interfoto, who ran a photographic transparency lending library, to enquire if they had any photographs of the 1950s. Interfoto, who had not done business with Stiletto before, said they would research Stiletto's request. Later that day Interfoto sent 47 transparencies packed in a jiffy bag to Stiletto. The bag contained a delivery note which stated in condition 2:

> All transparencies must be returned to us within 14 days from the date of posting/delivery/collection. A holding fee of £5 plus VAT per day will be charged for each transparency which is retained by you longer than the said period of 14 days . . .

Stiletto did not read the delivery note. Four weeks later Stiletto returned the transparencies to Interfoto. Interfoto then invoiced Stiletto for £3,783.50. Stiletto refused to pay and Interfoto brought an action against them to recover the £3,783.50.

Note that the 'usual' charge in the transparency lending business was less than £3.50 per slide per week.

The issues before the court were whether condition 2 had been incorporated into the contract and if so could Stiletto be relieved from liability under it.

Dillon LJ
The question is therefore whether condition 2 was sufficiently brought to the defendants' attention to make it a term of the contract which was only concluded after the defendants had received, and must have known that they had received the transparencies and the delivery note.

Condition 2 of these plaintiffs' conditions is in my judgment a very onerous clause. The defendants could not conceivably have known, if their attention was not drawn to the clause, that the plaintiffs were proposing to charge a 'holding fee' for the retention of the transparencies at such a very high and exorbitant rate.

. . . In the ticket cases the courts held that the common law required that reasonable steps be taken to draw the other parties' attention to the printed conditions or they would not be part of the contract. It is, in my judgment, a logical development of the common law into modern conditions that it should be held, as it was in *Thornton v Shoe Lane Parking Ltd*, that, if one condition in a set of printed conditions is particularly onerous or unusual, the party seeking to enforce it must show that that particular condition was fairly brought to the attention of the other party.

In the present case, nothing whatever was done by the plaintiffs to draw the defendants' attention particularly to condition 2; it was merely one of four columns' width of conditions printed across the foot of the delivery note. Consequently condition 2 never, in my judgment, became part of the contract between the parties.

10.4.6 Incorporation by course of dealing

Notice of the exclusion clause may be inferred into the contract from previous dealings.

Spurling Ltd v Bradshaw (1956)

The issue before the court was whether an exemption clause exempting Spurling had been incorporated into the contract.

Denning LJ

In the first part of June, 1953, the defendant bought eight wooden casks of orange juice, containing sixty gallons apiece. He bought them 'to clear for £120', and he sent them to some warehousemen, the plaintiffs, J Spurling, Ltd, who on June 10, 1953, sent a receipt for them, called a 'landing account', which said:

> 'We have pleasure in advising you that these goods consigned to you arrived at our premises this day and are subject to either warehouse, wharfage, demurrage or other charges . . . The company's conditions as printed on the back hereof cover the goods held in accordance with this notice. Goods will be insured if you instruct us accordingly; otherwise they are not insured.'

On the back there were 'Contract conditions' and many lines of small print, which included, towards the end, these words:

> 'We will not in any circumstances when acting either as warehousemen, wharfingers, contractors, stevedores, carriers by land, or agents, or in any other capacity, be liable for any loss, damage or detention howsoever, whensoever, or wheresoever occasioned in respect of any goods entrusted to or carried or handled by us in the course of our business, even when such loss, damage or detention may have been

occasioned by the negligence, wrongful act or default of ourselves or our servants or agents or others for whose acts we would otherwise be responsible.'

On the same date, June 10, 1953, the plaintiffs sent an invoice to the defendant: 'To receiving, warehousing and redelivery, £4', and there was a note at the bottom of it:

'All goods are handled by us in accordance with the conditions as over and warehoused at owner's risk and not insured unless specially instructed.'

There were no conditions 'as over' . . . The plaintiffs issued a writ for their charges amounting to £61 12 s 6d. The defendant put in a defence admitting the charges, but he also set up a counterclaim for £180 which, as I read it, was a counterclaim for negligence in the storage of the goods. He said that, when collected, five barrels were empty and without lids, one barrel contained dirty, water, and two barrels were leaking badly. The plaintiffs put in a defence to the counterclaim in which they denied the charge of negligence and further said it was an express term of the contract that they should not be liable for any loss or damage of or to in connection with the barrels, and they relied on the 'landing account' for that purpose. In all the circumstances, it was not surprising that the plaintiffs relied on the exempting clause . . .

This brings me to the question whether this clause was part of the contract. Counsel for the defendant urged us to hold that the plaintiffs did not do what was reasonably sufficient to give notice of the conditions within *Parker v South Eastern Ry Co*. I agree that the more unreasonable a clause is, the greater the notice which must be given of it. Some clauses which I have seen would need to be printed in red ink on the face of the document with a red hand pointing to it before the notice could be held to be sufficient. The clause in this case, however, in my judgment, does not call for such exceptional treatment, especially when it is construed, as it should be, subject to the proviso that it only applies when the warehouseman is carrying out his contract and not when he is deviating from it or breaking it in a radical respect. So construed, the judge was, I think, entitled to find that sufficient notice was given. It is to be noticed that the landing account on its face told the defendant that the goods would be insured if he gave instructions; otherwise they were not insured. The invoice, on its face, told him they were warehoused 'at owner's risk'. The printed conditions, when read subject to the proviso which I have mentioned, added little or nothing to those explicit statements taken together. Next it was said that the landing account and invoice were issued after the goods had been received and could not therefore be part of the contract of bailment: but the defendant admitted that he had received many landing accounts before. True he had not troubled to read them. On receiving this account, he took no objection to it, left the goods there, and went on paying the warehouse rent for months afterwards. It seems to me that by the course of business and conduct of the parties, these conditions were part of the contract.

In these circumstances, the plaintiffs were entitled to rely on this exempting condition. I think, therefore, that the counterclaim was properly dismissed, and this appeal also should be dismissed.

10.4.7 Invalid or inoperative exemption clauses

Even though an exemption clause exists one of the parties to the contract can themselves negate its effect.

Curtis v Chemical Cleaning & Dyeing Co Ltd (1951)

Curtis took a white satin wedding dress to the Chemical Cleaning and Dyeing Co's shop for cleaning. The shop assistant handed her a document headed 'Receipt' which she was asked to sign. Before doing so Curtis asked the assistant why her signature was required. She was told that it was because the shop would not accept liability for certain specified risks, including the risk of damage by or to the beads and sequins with which the dress was trimmed. Curtis then signed the 'receipt', which in fact stated 'This . . . article is accepted on condition that the company is not liable for any damage howsoever arising'. When the dress was returned to Curtis there was a stain on it. Curtis claimed that the shop had been negligent and brought an action against the shop claiming damages of £32 10s. The shop sought to rely on the exemption clause contained in the signed receipt.

The issue before the court was whether the oral assurance given by the shop assistant overrode the written agreement so as to negate or modify the exemption clause.

Lord Denning

This case is of importance because of the many cases nowadays when people sign printed forms without reading them, only to find afterwards that they contain stringent clauses exempting the other side from their common-law liabilities. In every such case it must be remembered that, if a person wishes to exempt himself from a liability which the common law imposes on him, he can only do it by an express stipulation brought home to the party affected, and assented to by him as part of the contract: *Olley v Marlborough Court*. If the party affected signs a written document, knowing it to be a contract which governs the relations between them, his signature is irrefragable evidence of his assent to the whole contract, including the exempting clauses, unless the signature is shown to be obtained by fraud or misrepresentation:

L'Estrange v Graucob. But what is a sufficient misrepresentation for this purpose?

In my opinion any behaviour, by words or conduct, is sufficient to be a misrepresentation if it is such as to mislead the other party about the existence or extent of the exemption. If it conveys a false impression, that is enough. If the false impression is created knowingly, it is a fraudulent misrepresentation; if it is created unwittingly, it is an innocent misrepresentation; but either is sufficient to disentitle the creator of it to the benefit of the exemption. . . . When one party puts forward a printed form for signature, failure by him to draw attention to the existence or extent of the exemption clause may in some circumstances convey the impression that there is no exemption at all, or at any rate not so wide an exemption as that which is in fact contained in the document. The present case is a good illustration. The customer said in evidence: 'When I was asked to sign the document I asked 'why? The assistant said I was to accept any responsibility for damage to beads and sequins. I did not read it all before I signed it'. In those circumstances, by failing to draw attention to the width of the exemption clause, the assistant created the false impression that the exemption only related to the beads and sequins, and that it did not extend to the material of which the dress was made. It was done perfectly innocently, but nevertheless a false impression was created . . . [I]t was a sufficient misrepresentation to disentitle the cleaners from relying on the exemption, except in regard to beads and sequins.

. . . In my opinion when the signature to a condition, purporting to exempt a person from his common-law liabilities, is obtained by an innocent misrepresentation, the party who has made that misrepresentation is disentitled to rely on the exemption . . .

10.4.8 Overriding oral undertaking

Another way in which an exemption clause can be negated by one of the parties to the contract is if they themselves make an oral representation to the other party which contradicts the exemption clause.

Evans & Son (Portsmouth) Ltd v Andrea Merzario Ltd (1976)

For many years Evans had employed Andrea, who were forwarding agents, to arrange for their goods to be transported by sea to England. Up until 1967 Andrea had always had Evans goods shipped below deck. In 1967 Andrea suggested to Evans that in future Evans' goods should be transported in containers. Evans agreed to this provided that their goods continued to be shipped below decks. Andrea gave Evans an oral assurance that the containers would be so shipped. A container containing Evans' goods was wrongly shipped on deck. During the voyage the container was lost overboard. Evans claimed damages against Andrea for loss of their goods alleging that Andrea was in breach of contract in not having had the goods shipped below decks. The written agreement between Evans and Andrea contained condition 11 which stated that Andrea would not be liable for loss or damage unless it occurred whilst in their actual custody and then only if they were guilty of wilful neglect or default. Condition 13 of the agreement stated that Andrea's liability was not to exceed the value of the goods or a sum at the rate of £50 per ton of 20 cwt.

The issue before the court was whether Andrea could rely on conditions 11 and 13.

Lord Denning MR

... When a person gives a promise, or an assurance to another, intending that he should act on it by entering into a contract, and he does act on it by entering into the contract, we hold that it is binding ... Following this approach, it seems to me plain that [Andrea] gave an oral promise or assurance that the goods in this new container traffic would be carried under deck. He made the promise in order to induce [Evans] to agree to the goods being carried in containers. On the faith of it, [Evans] accepted the quotations and gave orders for transport. In those circumstances the promise was binding. There was a breach of that promise and the forwarding agents are liable – unless they can rely on the printed conditions.

It is common ground that the course of dealing was on the standard conditions of the forwarding trade. Those conditions were relied on. Condition 4 which gives the company complete freedom in respect of means, route and procedure in the transportation of goods. Condition 11 which says that the company will not be liable for loss or damage unless it occurs whilst in their actual custody and then only if they are guilty of wilful neglect or default. Condition 13 which says that their liability shall not exceed the value of the goods or a sum at the rate of £50 per ton of 20 cwt. The question is whether the company can rely on those exemptions. I do not think so. The cases are numerous in which oral promises have been held binding in spite of written exempting conditions ... Following these authorities, it seems to me that the forwarding agents cannot rely on the condition. There was a plain breach of the oral promise by the forwarding agents. I would allow the appeal.

10.5 Summary

In this section you've seen:

- that an exemption clause can be incorporated into a contract by signature: see *L'Estrange v Graucob Ltd* (1934).
- that an exemption clause can be incorporated into a contract by

reasonable notice. Whether reasonable notice been given depends on the nature of document – was the document intended to have contractual force?: see *Chapelton v Barry UDC* (1940).

- that if a document was not obviously a contractual document then the person relying on the exemption clause must show that the other party was given reasonable notice that the document contained conditions?: see *Parker v South Eastern Railway Co* (1877).

- that the party relying on the exemption clause need not show that he has actually brought it to the notice of the other party, but only that he took reasonable steps to do so, see *Parker v South Eastern Railway Co* (1877).

- that notice of the exemption clause must be given before the contract has been made? see *Olley v Marlborough Court* (1949).

- that reasonableness of notice depends on extent of exclusion: see *Interfoto Picture Library Ltd v Stiletto Visual Programmes Ltd* (1988).

- that notice of the exemption clause may in inferred from previous course of dealings: see *Spurling v Bradshaw* (1956).

- that even though an exemption clause exists the party who seeks to rely on it can himself render it of no effect by, for example, misrepresenting the effect of the exemption clause: see *Curtis v Chemical Cleaning & Dyeing Co Ltd* (1951).

Chapter 11

Unfair Contract Terms
Act 1977

CONTENTS

11.1 Introduction

This chapter deals with the statutory provisions that apply to exemption clauses. The chapter will examine how the Unfair Contract Terms Act 1977 (UCTA) applies to some exemption clauses. We will see how UCTA distinguishes between exemption clauses rendered void and those needing to satisfy the 'reasonableness test'. We will also see how the 'reasonableness test' is applied to contracts to which UCTA applies.

11.1.1 Scope of the Unfair Contract Terms Act 1977 (UCTA)

1 The Act does not apply to regulate all contract terms but generally only those that attempt to exclude or restrict liability.
2 Most provisions of the Act only apply to the exclusion of 'business liability' (as defined in s 1(3)).
   Section 1(3) states:

> In the case of ... contract ..., sections 2 to 7 apply ... only to
> business liability, that is liability for breach of obligations or duties
> arising–
>
> (a) from things done or to be done by a person in the course of a
>   business (whether his own business or another's); or
> (b) from the occupation of premises used for business purposes of the
>   occupier;
>
> and references to liability are to be read accordingly . . .

3 Schedule 1 of the Act provides that certain contracts are not covered
by the Act's provisions, for example, contracts of employment, contracts of
insurance and carriage of goods by sea.

If the Act does apply, **some** exclusion clauses are rendered **void** by the
Act **while some** are merely subjected to a **requirement of reasonableness**.

11.2 Contracts for the sale of goods

11.2.1 Exclusion clauses rendered VOID under UCTA

Section 6(1) states that liability for breach of the obligations arising from
s 12 of the Sale of Goods Act 1979 (seller's implied undertakings as to
title) **cannot** be excluded or restricted by reference to any contract term.

Section 6(2) states that as against a person dealing as consumer (see
below), liability for breach of the obligations arising from ss 13, 14 or 15 of
the Sale of Goods Act 1979 (seller's implied undertakings as to conformity
of goods with description or sample, or as to their quality or fitness for a
particular purpose) **cannot** be excluded or restricted by reference to any
contract term.

11.2.2 Exclusion clauses subject to reasonableness

Section 6(3) states that as against a person dealing **otherwise than as consumer**
liability for breach of the obligations arising from ss 13, 14 or 15 of the
Sale of Goods Act 1979 **can be excluded** or restricted by reference to a contract term, but only in so far as the term satisfies the requirement of
reasonableness.

11.3 Contracts generally

11.3.1 Clauses subject to reasonableness

Section 3 states that where one of the parties (say Alice), **deals as consumer**, or **on the other's written standard terms of business,**[1] the other party (say Big Co Ltd) cannot, by reference to any contract term, exclude or restrict any liability of his (namely, Big Co Ltd's liability) in respect of the breach except in so far the contract term satisfies the requirement of reasonableness.

Section 12 states that a party to a contract **'deals as consumer'** in relation to another party if he:

> . . . neither makes the contract in the course of a business, and
> the other party does make the contract in the course of a business.

You might therefore think that if one business was to buy goods from another business that s 3 would not apply because neither party would be 'dealing as a consumer': you'd be wrong!

Remember s 3 states that where one of the parties (say this time Little Co Ltd) deals on the other's **written standard terms of business** (say Big Co Ltd) the other party cannot (i.e. Big Co Ltd), by reference to any contract term, exclude or restrict any liability of his (i.e. Big Co Ltd's liability) in respect of the breach except in so far the contract term satisfies the requirement of reasonableness.

Peter Symmons & Co v Cook (1981)

Peter Symmons & Co, a firm of surveyors, bought a Rolls Royce from Cook, a car dealer, for £9,000. The mileage of the car was 62,000 miles. Within 2,000 miles of its being bought the car was found to be suffering from a number of things wrong with it. It was in such a condition that it was cheaper to replace it than repair it.

Peter Symmons & Co claimed damages from Cook on the grounds that:

---

1   *The Chester Grosvenor Hotel Co Ltd v Alfred McAlpine Management Ltd* (1991)

Judge Stannard

The question of what are 'written standard terms of business' [in s 3 of UCTA] is one of fact and degree. Where a party contracts invariably in the same written terms without material variation, those terms will become its 'standard form contract' or 'written standard terms of business'. However, those terms need not be employed invariably or without material variation, and what is required for terms to be standard is that they should be regarded by the party which advances them as its standard terms and that it should habitually contract in those terms. If it contracts also in other terms or substantially modifies those terms it is a question of fact as to whether this has occurred so frequently or those terms have been altered so substantially that they must be regarded as not having been employed on that occasion.

(1) he had warranted that the car was in excellent condition (an express term);

(2) he was in breach of the implied condition set out in s 14(2) Sale of Goods Act 1893, in that the car was not of merchantable quality (an implied term); and

(3) he was also in breach of the implied condition set out in s 14(3) Sale of Goods Act 1893 in that the car was not reasonably fit for its purpose (another implied term).

Cook denied that any express warranty had been given, and contended that the implied conditions set out in the Sale of Goods Act 1893 did not apply because the sale was a non-consumer sale and they were therefore excluded by virtue of s 6 Unfair Contract Terms Act 1977 as they had been expressly disclaimed.

The issue before the court was whether Peter Symmons & Co was 'dealing as a consumer'.

The court held Peter Symmons & Co **were** 'dealing as consumers'!

Mr R Rougier QC, sitting as a deputy judge said:

> There would be judgment for S & Co for £4,000. On the evidence, S & Co were 'dealing as consumers' within the meaning of s 12 Unfair Contract Terms Act 1977 and their rights under the Sale of Goods Act 1893 could not be excluded. For a sale to fall outside the category of a consumer sale by virtue of S & Co's buying in the course of business, the buying of cars must form at the very least an integral part of the buyer's business or a necessary incidental thereto. Only in those circumstances could the buyer be said to be on an equal footing with the seller. There was a breach of the express warranty that the car was in excellent condition. The car was not of merchantable quality nor reasonably fit for the purpose.

Despite the fact that Peter Symmons & Co appeared NOT to be 'dealing as a consumer' (they SEEMED TO BE 'BUYING IN THE COURSE OF A BUSINESS') on the evidence, Peter Symmons & Co were 'dealing as consumers' within the meaning of s 12 Unfair Contract Terms Act 1977 and their rights under the Sale of Goods Act 1893 (as it then was) could not be excluded.

Peter Symmons & Co v Cook establishes that what s 12 is looking for is not who is buying the goods but in what **capacity** is the buyer buying the goods.

It is irrelevant for the purposes of s 12 that the buyer is a business.

The test is whether the buyer is buying the goods as an 'integral part of the buyer's business'.

In *Peter Symmons & Co v Cook* was a Rolls Royce an 'integral part of Peter Symmons & Co business'?

NB If Peter Symmons & Co had bought a Land Rover then the court may well have held that a Land Rover was an 'integral part of their business' as a surveyor.

R & B Customs Brokers Co Ltd v United Dominions Trust Ltd (1988)

This case develops the definition of 'dealing as a consumer'.

R & B Customs Brokers (a two-man company) occasionally bought second-hand cars from United Dominions Trust Ltd (UDT). On one occasion they bought a second-hand Colt Shogun car from UDT for their business. The car turned out to suffer from a serious leak which could not be repaired. R & B Customs Brokers sought to reject the car on the ground that the car was not of merchantable quality within the meaning of s 14(2) of the Sale of Goods Act 1979 or fit for the purpose within the meaning of s 14(3) of the Sale of Goods Act 1979. The Court of Appeal having decided that the car was not fit for its purpose then had to decide whether an exclusion clause in the contract excluding United Dominions Trust Ltd's liability was effective. This depended on whether R & B Customs Brokers, a company, had dealt 'as a consumer'.

The issue before the court was whether R & B Customs Brokers had dealt 'as a consumer'.

The court held R & B Customs Brokers were 'dealing as consumers'!

Despite the fact that R & B Customs Brokers had bought several cars for their business – which arguably amounted to buying as an integral part of the business the court held that where an activity MERELY INCIDENTAL to the carrying on of a business A DEGREE OF REGULARITY had to be established before it could be said that the activity was AN INTEGRAL PART OF THE BUSINESS and so CARRIED ON IN THE COURSE OF THAT BUSINESS.

On the facts, the necessary degree of regularity had not been shown.

Therefore, the company was DEALING AS A CONSUMER within the meaning of s 12(1) Unfair Contract Terms Act 1977, and by virtue of s 6(2) of that Act the implied term of fitness for purpose could not be excluded.

St Albans City and District Council v ICL (1996)

St Albans City and District Council (the Council) purchased hardware and software from International Computers Limited (ICL). As a result of a computer error the Council suffered a loss of £1,314,846. The judge, Scott Baker J, having found ICL in 'plain breach of contract' went on to consider whether ICL could rely on an exemption clause, which read:

> In all other cases ICL's liability will not exceed the price, or charge payable for the item of equipment, program or service in respect of which the liability arises or £100,000 (whichever is the lesser). Provided that in no event will ICL be liable for–

(1) loss resulting from any defect, or deficiency which ICL shall have physically remedied at its own expense within a reasonable time; or
(2) any indirect or consequential loss or loss of business, or profits sustained by the customer; or
(3) loss which could have been avoided by the customer following ICL's reasonable advice and instructions.

On appeal the question before the court was did the Council deal on ICL's written standard terms of business?

The court held that St Albans City and District Council dealt on ICL's written standard terms for the purposes of s 3(1).

Nourse LJ
I come finally to the Unfair Contract Terms Act 1977. As I have said, the judge found that the contract incorporated the defendant's general conditions of contract for the supply of equipment, programmes and services. It has not been suggested that those conditions were not written standard terms of business for the purposes of the 1977 Act.

. . . The first question is whether, as between the plaintiffs and the defendant, the plaintiffs dealt as consumer or on the defendant's written standard terms of business within section 3(1). In the light of section 12(1)(a) and the definition of 'business' in section 14, it is accepted on behalf of the plaintiffs that they did not deal as consumer. So the question is reduced to this. Did the plaintiffs 'deal' on the defendant's written standard terms of business?

[Council for ICL] submitted that the question must be answered in the negative, on the ground that you cannot be said to deal on another's standard terms of business if, as was here the case, you negotiate with him over those terms before you enter into the contract. In my view that is an impossible construction for two reasons: first, because as a matter of plain English 'deals' means 'makes a deal', irrespective of any negotiations that may have preceded it; secondly, because section 12(1)(a) equates the expression 'deals as consumer' with 'makes the contract'. Thus it is clear that in order that one of the contracting parties may deal on the other's written standard terms of business within section 3(1) it is only necessary for him to enter into the contract on those terms . . .

[In the High Court] Mr Justice Scott Baker dealt with this question as one of fact, finding that the defendant's general conditions remained effectively untouched in the negotiations and that the plaintiffs accordingly dealt on the defendant's written standard terms for the purposes of section 3(1). I respectfully agree with him. The consequence of that finding is that the defendant cannot rely on clause 9(c) except in so far as it satisfies the requirement of reasonableness . . . [T]he judge carefully considered that question and held that clause 9(c) did not pass that test.

11.4 The requirement of reasonableness

The reasonableness test is laid down in s 11.

Section 11 states that a term shall have been a fair and reasonable one to have been included in a contract having regard to the circumstances which were, or ought reasonably to have been, known to or in the contemplation of the parties when the contract was made.

NB Where the 'exclusion clause' seeks to restrict liability to a specified sum of money, and the question arises whether the term or notice satisfies the requirement of reasonableness, regard shall be had to the resources which he could expect to be available to him for the purpose of meeting the liability should it arise and how far it was open to him to cover himself by insurance (s 11(4)).

NB It is for those claiming that a contract term satisfies the requirement of reasonableness to show that it does (s 11(5)).

George Mitchell (Chesterhall) Ltd v Finney Lock Seeds Ltd (1983)
Finney Lock sold cabbage seed to George Mitchell for £201. The contract contained a clause which stated:

> [1] In the event of any seeds ... proving defective ... we will, at our option, replace the defective seeds ... free of charge to the buyer or will refund all payments made to us by the buyer ... [2] We hereby exclude all liability for any loss or damage arising from the use of any seeds ... supplied by us and for any consequential loss or damage ...

George Mitchell planted 63 acres with the seeds. The crop was useless and had to be ploughed in. George Mitchell brought an action against Finney Lock claiming damages of £61,513 for breach of contract.

The issue before the court was whether the exemption clause was 'fair or reasonable' within the meaning of s 11?

The court held that the exclusion clause was NOT a 'fair or reasonable one' within the meaning of s 11.

Lord Bridge of Harwich

The question of relative bargaining strength under para (a) and of the opportunity to buy seeds without a limitation of the seedsman's liability under para (b) were interrelated. The evidence was that a similar limitation of liability was universally embodied in the terms of trade between seedsmen and farmers and had been so for very many years. The limitation had never been negotiated between representative bodies but, on the other hand, had not been the subject of any protest by the National Farmers' Union. These factors, if considered in isolation, might have been equivocal. The decisive factor, however, appears from the evidence of four witnesses called for the appellants, two independent seedsmen, the chairman of the appellant company, and a director of a sister company (both being wholly-owned subsidiaries of the same parent). They said that it had always been their practice, unsuccessfully attempted in the instant case, to negotiate settlements of farmers' claims for damages in excess of the price of the seeds, if they thought that the claims were 'genuine' and 'justified'. This evidence indicated a clear recognition by seedsmen in general, and the appellants in particular, that reliance on the limitation of liability imposed by the relevant condition would not be fair or reasonable.

... Finally, as the trial judge found, seedsmen could insure against the risk of crop failure caused by supply of the wrong variety of seeds without materially increasing the price of seeds.

... I should conclude without hesitation that it would not be fair or reasonable to allow the appellants to rely on the contractual limitation of their liability.

RW Green Ltd v Cade Bros Farms (1978)

Green sold 20 tons of uncertified seed potatoes to Cade for £634. When the potatoes began to grow it became obvious that they were infected with a potato virus. As a result of this virus infection the crop was very poor. Cade claimed that the seed potatoes had not been of merchantable quality or fit for their purpose within the meaning of s 14 of the Sale of Goods Act 1893 and they claimed damages for loss of profit of £6,000. Green replied that their liability was limited to the price of the potatoes – £634 – by clause 5 of the contract of sale which provided:

> ... Time being the essence of this Contract ... notification of rejection, claim or complaint must be made to the Seller giving a statement of the grounds for such rejection claim or complaint within three days ... after the arrival of the seed at its destination ... It is specifically provided and agreed that compensation and damages payable under any claim or claims arising out of this Contract under whatsoever pretext shall not under any circumstances amount in aggregate to more than the Contract price of the potatoes forming the subject of the claim or claims.

The issue before the court was whether the exemption clause was 'fair or reasonable' within the meaning of s 11?

The court held that the exclusion clause **was a 'fair and reasonable one'** within the meaning of s 11.

The court said:

Griffiths J

Should I exercise my discretion under [s. 6] and declare it to be unenforceable, because it would not be fair or reasonable to let the plaintiffs rely upon it?

I have considered the matters to which I am particularly directed to have regard by [s 11], in so far as they are relevant in this case. The parties were of equal bargaining strength; the buyer received no inducement to accept the term. True, it appears that he could not easily have bought potatoes without this term in the contract, but he had had the protection of the National Farmers' Union to look after his interests as the contract evolved and he knew that he was trading on these conditions.

No moral blame attaches to either party; neither of them knew, nor could be expected to know, that the potatoes were infected. There was of course a risk; it was a risk that the farmer could largely have avoided by buying certified seed, but he chose not to do so. To my mind the contract in clear language places the risk in so far as damage may exceed the contract price, on the farmer. The contract has been in use for many years with the approval of the negotiating bodies acting on behalf of both seed potato merchants and farmers, and I can see no grounds upon which it would be right for the Court to say in the circumstances of this case that such a term is not fair or reasonable.

11.5 Third parties, exclusion clauses and Contracts (Rights of Third Parties) Act 1999

If a contract makes it clear that the benefit that the third party is to receive is the right to rely on an exclusion clause then in any action by one of the parties to the contract against the third party, the third party can rely on the exclusion clause (see s 1(6) Contracts (Rights of Third Parties) Act 1999).

This is an important provision especially as regards the ability of subcontractors to exclude or restrict their liability against the main contractor.

For example, Anne contracts with Brenda to build Brenda a house. Brenda employs subcontractors to carry out parts of the building work. Before the Act Brenda could exclude her liability to Anne but the subcontractors could not exclude their liability in negligence to Anne because there was no contract between them and Anne. Now when Brenda enters into a contract with Anne she can include a term in the contract which excludes or limits the liability of the subcontractors to Brenda.

11.6 Unfair Terms in Consumer Contracts Regulations 1999

These, to a large extent, duplicate the provisions of UCTA.

11.7 Summary

In this section you've seen:

- that the Unfair Contract Terms Act 1977 does not apply to regulate any contract term, but generally only those that attempt to exclude or restrict liability.
- that most provisions of the Unfair Contract Terms Act 1977 only apply to the exclusion of 'business liability' as defined in s 1(3).
- that certain contracts are not covered by the Unfair Contract Terms Act 1977, for example, contracts of employment, contracts of insurance, carriage of goods by sea – see the Unfair Contract Terms Act 1977, Sched 1.
- that if the Unfair Contract Terms Act 1977 does apply, some exclusion clauses are rendered void by the Act, while some are merely subjected to a requirement of reasonableness.
- that exclusion clauses which purport to exclude liability for breach of implied conditions in ss 12–15 of the Sale of Goods Act 1979 (title, description, satisfactory quality, fitness for purpose, correspondence with sample) where the buyer deals as a consumer (**NB** s 6(1) applies to ALL sales) are rendered VOID under s 6(1) and (2) of the Unfair Contract Terms Act 1977.
- that exclusion clauses which purport to exclude liability for description, quality, fitness or sample where the other does not deal as a consumer are subject to the test of reasonableness under s 6(3) of the Unfair Contract Terms Act 1977.
- that exclusion clauses which purport to exclude contractual liability where one party deals as a consumer or on the other's written standard terms of business are subject to the test of reasonableness under s 3 of the Unfair Contract Terms Act 1977.
- that a business deals as a consumer if the goods it purchases do not form 'at the very least an integral part of the buyer's business or a necessary incidental thereto': see *Peter Symmons & Co v Cook* (1981).
- that where an activity is merely incidental to the carrying on of a business a degree of regularity has to be established before it can be said that the activity is an integral part of the business: see *R & B Customs Brokers Co Ltd v United Dominions Trust Ltd* (1988).
- that the question of what are 'written standard terms of business' is one of fact and degree: see *The Chester Grosvenor Hotel Co Ltd v Alfred McAlpine Management Ltd* (1991).

Chapter 12

Misrepresentation

12.1 Introduction

Misrepresentation deals with the situation where somebody makes an untrue statement to the innocent party which induces that party to enter into a contract with them. If that untrue statement has become a term of the contract, the innocent party's remedy will be for breach of contract. However, and this is where misrepresentation comes in, what if that statement has not become a term of the contract? In such a case the innocent party's remedy will not be for breach of contract, because no term of the contract will have been broken, but the remedy will be for misrepresentation. In this chapter we will identify what amounts to a false representation of fact, and the identity of the person to whom the misrepresentation was addressed. We will also consider whether that misrepresentation actually induced the innocent party to enter into the contract. Finally, we will examine the remedies available to the misled person.

12.2 Misrepresentation – explained

A misrepresentation is not part of a contract!

It is made before the contract is made. Really misrepresentation is the Tort of Deceit.

Definition

An operative misrepresentation consists of a false statement of existing or past fact made by one party before or at the time of making the contract, which is addressed to the other party and which induces the other party to enter into the contract.

NB Misrepresentation is necessary to cover the situation where:

- some statement is made to you before you enter into a contract with the person who made the statement;
- that statement influences you in deciding to enter into the contract; and
- that statement is not included in the contract (if it was included in the contract and it turned out to be false you could sue for breach of contract).

For example, you go to buy a second-hand car. The car dealer tells you an elderly widow who has never driven it at more than 50 miles per hour has owned the car since new. That statement influences you into buying the car. You later find out that the car had five previous owners, the last one being a young teenager who used the car for drag racing.

Can you force the car dealer to take the car back?

If the car dealer's statement about the ownership had become a term of the contract then you could sue him for breach of a term of the contract.

However, it is most unlikely that the statement would have become a term of the contract. This is where misrepresentation comes in. You could sue the car dealer for misrepresentation. Your remedy would be to bring the contract to an end and force him to take the car back and repay you your purchase price.

12.3 The representation

There must be a false representation of fact. A statement of opinion is not (usually) a statement of fact.

Bisset v Wilkinson (1927)

Wilkinson agreed to buy a farm from Bisset. During the negotiations Bisset, who had only used a small part of the farm as a sheep farm, told Wilkinson that:

> . . . if the place was worked as I was working it . . . my idea was that it would carry two thousand sheep.

Before the court Bisset said:

> I do not dispute that (Wilkinson) bought it believing it would carry the two thousand sheep.

Wilkinson claimed that Bisset's statement as to the carrying capacity of the farm was a misrepresentation and that, therefore, he was entitled to have the contract rescinded.

The issue before the court was whether Bisset's statement amounted to a misrepresentation.

The court held that Bisset's statement was NOT a misrepresentation DESPITE BEING INACCURATE.

Since Bisset had not farmed sheep on the land, and Wilkinson KNEW this, Bisset's statement was only an expression of opinion, and not a statement of fact.

12.4 A statement of opinion can – exceptionally – constitute a representation of fact

Smith v Land and House Property Corp (1884)

Smith advertised a hotel for sale. It was described as:

> . . . now held by a very desirable tenant, Mr Frederick Fleck, for an unexpired term of twenty-eight years, at a rent of £400 per annum.

In fact Fleck, who had been a tenant from 1880, had paid no rent until January 1882. Further, Fleck had only paid part of the last quarter's rent and then only under threat of distress. On discovering the true character of Fleck the Land and House Property Corporation, who had agreed to buy the hotel, refused to complete. Smith sued them for specific performance (that is, sued them to perform the contract as agreed) and the Land and House Property

Corporation claimed that the contract should be rescinded on the ground of Smith's misrepresentation as to the character of Fleck.

The issue before the court was whether Smith's statement was a misrepresentation of fact or opinion.

The court held that Smith's statement was a misrepresentation of FACT.

The 'OPINION' was based on existing fact – that the rent had not been paid – and that 'opinion' could not have been logically reached from those facts.

12.5 Advertising 'puffs' are not representations of fact

Dimmock v Hallett (1866)
At a sale by auction, Dimmock described his land to be 'fertile and improvable'; it was in fact partly abandoned and useless.

The issue before the court was whether Dimmock's statement was a misrepresentation of fact or a flourishing description.

The court held that Dimmock's words were 'a mere flourishing description by an auctioneer'.

Turner LJ

The purchaser further grounds his case on misrepresentation in the particulars. Some of the instances alleged appear to me to be unimportant. Thus I think that a mere general statement that land is fertile and improvable, whereas part of it has been abandoned as useless, cannot, except in extreme cases – as, for instance, where a considerable part is covered with water, or otherwise irreclaimable – be considered such a misrepresentation as to entitle a purchaser to be discharged. In the present case, I think the statement is to be looked at as a mere flourishing description by an auctioneer.

12.6 Positive statement or conduct required in order to amount to an operative misrepresentation

There must be some positive statement or conduct in order to amount to an operative misrepresentation.

There is **no duty to disclose** anything to the other party, **but if you do it must be the full truth**.

Dimmock v Hallett (1866) (continued)
Hallett purchased an estate consisting of several farms from Dimmock. The particulars of sale described the farms as being fully let. On taking possession of the estate Hallett found that two of the tenants who had been

described as continuing tenants had given notice to quit their farms. Hallett claimed that the statement that the farms were fully let amounted to a misrepresentation by Dimmock and that, therefore, the contract of sale should be rescinded on the grounds of misrepresentation.

The issue before the court was whether Dimmock's statement was a misrepresentation of fact or opinion.

The court held that Dimmock's statement was a misrepresentation of FACT.

Hallett was led to suppose that the farms that he was purchasing had continuing tenancies at fixed rents.

Turner LJ

The Court requires good faith in conditions of sale, and looks strictly at the statements contained in them . . . there is no reference made in the particulars to the fact that each of these tenants had given a notice to quit . . . The purchaser, therefore, would be led to suppose, as to these farms, that he was purchasing with continuing tenancies at fixed rents, whereas he would, in fact, have to find tenants immediately after the completion of his purchase. This . . . seems to me, is a material misrepresentation . . .

I am of opinion, therefore, that (Hallett) is entitled to be discharged.

12.7 A mere silence is not a misrepresentation

Keates v Lord Cadogan (1851)
The Earl of Cadogan let a house which he knew to be

> . . . in such a ruinous and dangerous state and condition as to be dangerous to enter, occupy, or dwell in, and was likely wholly or in part to fall down, and thereby do damage and injury to persons and property therein . . .

to Keates for three years at an annual rent of £5. Keates argued that the contract should be set aside on the ground that the Earl of Cadogan should have warned him of the state of the house before he agreed to rent it.

The issue before the court was whether Lord Cadogan's failure to inform Keates of the condition of the house amounted to a misrepresentation.

The court held that Keates could not sue Lord Cadogan.

The court said that there was no warranty that the house was fit for immediate occupation.

Jervis CJ

I do not think that this declaration discloses a sufficient cause of action. It is not contended that there was any warranty that the house was fit for immediate occupation: but it is said, that because the defendant knows it is in a ruinous state, and does nothing to inform the plaintiff of that fact, therefore the action is maintainable. It is consistent with the state of things disclosed in the declaration, that, the defendant knowing the state of things, the plaintiff may have come to him and said, 'Will you lease that house to me?' and the defendant may have answered 'Yes, I will.' It is not contended by the plaintiff that any misrepresentation was made; nor was it alleged that the plaintiff was acting on the impression produced by the conduct of the defendant as to the state of the house, or that he was not to make investigations before he began to reside in it. I think, therefore, that the defendant is entitled to our judgment, there being no obligation on the defendant to say anything about the state of the house, and no allegation of deceit. It is an ordinary case of letting.

12.8 What if circumstances change?

What if something is true when it is first said but because of changed circumstances it becomes untrue?

With v O'Flanagan (1936)

In January 1934, With entered into negotiations with Dr O'Flanagan to purchase his medical practice. At that time Dr O'Flanagan said that the business had takings of £2,000 per year. However, when With purchased the business in May 1934 the takings had fallen to £5 per week due to the illness of Dr O'Flanagan; this fact had not been disclosed to With. On discovering this fact With sought to have the contract rescinded on the grounds of Dr O'Flanagan's misrepresentation.

The question before the court was whether O'Flanagan's failure to inform With of the changes in circumstances amounted to a misrepresentation.

The court held that With COULD sue O'Flanagan.

The court said that since With had entered into the contract in ignorance of that change of circumstances and had relied upon that representation O'Flanagan couldn't hold With to the bargain.

Romer LJ

The only principle invoked by the appellants in this case is as follows. If A. with a view to inducing B. to enter into a contract makes a representation as to a material fact, then if at a later date and before the contract is actually entered into, owing to a change of circumstances, the representation then made would to the knowledge of A. be untrue and B. subsequently enters into the contract in ignorance of that change of circumstances and relying upon that representation, A. cannot hold B. to the bargain. There is ample authority for that statement and, indeed, I doubt myself whether any authority is necessary, it being, it seems to me, so obviously consistent with the plainest principles of equity.

12.9 The representation must be addressed to the party misled

Peek v Gurney (1873)

The promoters of a company were sued by Peek who had purchased shares on the faith of false statements contained in a prospectus issued by them. Peek was not a person to whom shares had been allotted on the first formation of the company; he had merely purchased shares on the stock exchange.

The issue before the court was whether the company promoters had made a misrepresentation to Peek.

The court held that as the prospectus was ONLY ADDRESSED TO THE FIRST APPLICANTS for shares; that it could NOT be supposed to EXTEND TO OTHERS than these; and that on the allotment 'the prospectus had done its work; it was exhausted'.

In other words, although there had been a misrepresentation IT WAS NOT ADDRESSED to Peek. It was not intended to mislead him.

12.10 The representation must induce the contract

Although the representation must induce the innocent party to enter into the contract, there is no need to prove that contract was made because of the representation.

Smith v Chadwick (1884)

Lord Blackburn
I think that if it is proved that the defendant with a view to induce the plaintiff to enter into a contract made a statement to the plaintiff of such a nature as would be likely to induce a person to enter into a contract, and it is proved that the plaintiff did enter into the contract, it is a fair inference of fact that he was induced to do so by the statement.

12.11 Opportunities for inspection

The mere fact that the misled party has had the opportunity of investigating and ascertaining whether the representation is true or false will not necessarily deprive him of his right to allege that he was deceived by it.

Redgrave v Hurd (1881)

Redgrave, an elderly solicitor, advertised for a partner 'who would not object to purchase advertiser's suburban residence, suitable for a family, value £1600'. Hurd answered the advertisement and enquired as to the income of the practice. Redgrave told him that the business brought in about £300 per year and showed him receipts amounting to about £200. When Hurd asked how the remaining £100 was made up Redgrave showed him a number of papers which he said related to other business not included in the summaries. These papers, which Hurd did not examine, showed only a most trifling amount of business. Hurd shortly afterwards signed an agreement to purchase the house for £1600, and paid a deposit. Hurd took possession, but finding that the business was worthless, refused to complete. Redgrave brought an action for specific performance against Hurd. Hurd put in a defence, in which he disputed the right to specific performance on the ground of misrepresentations as to the business, and by counter-claim claimed on the same ground to have the contract rescinded, and to have damages on the ground of the expenses he had been put to and the loss incurred by giving up his own practice.

The issue before the court was whether Hurd have relied on Redgrave's representation as to the practice's income since he had the means of discovering, and might, with reasonable diligence, have discovered that Redgrave's representation was untrue.

The court held that Hurd was under no obligation to check the accuracy of Redgrave's statements even though he had the means to do so.

> **Jessel MR**
>
> If a man is induced to enter into a contract by a false representation it is not a sufficient answer to him to say, 'If you had used due diligence you would have found out that the statement was untrue. You had the means afforded you of discovering its falsity, and did not choose to avail yourself of them.'

12.12 Remedies for misrepresentation

The remedies available for misrepresentation depend upon the type of misrepresentation.

There are three types of misrepresentation:

* fraudulent
* negligent and
* innocent misrepresentation.

12.12.1 Fraudulent misrepresentation

In practice, fraudulent misrepresentation is not made use of these days, so it isn't dealt with in this book.

12.12.2 Negligent misrepresentation

Although this type of misrepresentation is commonly known as negligent misrepresentation, it is more accurately referred to as 'misrepresentation under s 2(1) of the Misrepresentation Act 1967' – but that's not as catchy a name!

Section 2(1) states:

> Where a person has entered into a contract after a misrepresentation has been made to him by another party thereto and as a result thereof he has suffered loss, that person shall be so liable, unless he proves that he had reasonable ground to believe and did believe up to the time the contract was made that the facts represented were true.

Howard Marine & Dredging Co Ltd v Ogden & Sons (Excavations) Ltd (1978)

Howards told Ogden that their barges would each carry about 1,600 tonnes. Relying on this statement Ogden hired the two barges from Howards. In fact the barges would only carry 1,055 tonnes. In making their statement Howards was relying on the figure they remembered seeing in Lloyd's Register. In fact the figure in Lloyd's Register was wrong. The barges' own shipping documents, which Howards had in their possession and had read, clearly showed that the barges would only carry 1,055 tonnes. On discovering the misrepresentation Ogden refused to pay the hire and Howards withdrew the barges and sued for the outstanding payments. Ogden counter-claimed and claimed damages under s 2(1) Misrepresentation Act 1967.

Was Ogden successful in his claim? The court held that Howards had failed to prove that they had reasonable ground to believe the truth of their misrepresentation to Ogden and accordingly they were liable under s 2(1) to Ogden.

Bridge LJ

I will consider first the position under [s 2(1) of] the statute.

The judge found in terms that what [Howards] said about the capacity of the barges was said with the object of getting the hire contract for Howards, in other words with the intention that it should be acted on. This was clearly right. Equally clearly the misrepresentation was in fact acted on by Ogdens. It follows, therefore, on the plain language of the 1967 Act that Howards must be liable unless they proved that [they] had reasonable ground to believe what he said about the barges' capacity.

. . . If the representee proves a misrepresentation . . . the onus passes immediately to the representor to prove that he had reasonable ground to believe the facts represented . . . the 1967 Act imposes an absolute obligation not to state facts which the representor cannot prove he had reasonable ground to believe.

. . . [I]t is to be assumed that [Howards] was perfectly honest throughout. But the question remains whether [their] evidence, however benevolently viewed, is sufficient to show that [they] had an objectively reasonable ground to disregard the figure in the ship's documents and to prefer the

Lloyd's Register figure. I think it is not . . . Accordingly I conclude that Howards failed to prove that [they] had reasonable ground to believe the truth of [their] misrepresentation to [Ogden].

12.12.3 Innocent misrepresentation

Definition

An innocent misrepresentation is a misrepresentation where no element of fraud or negligence is present.

12.12.3.1 Remedies available for innocent misrepresentation

12.12.3.1.1 DAMAGES

Damages are NOT AVAILABLE for an innocent misrepresentation.

12.12.3.1.2 RESCISSION

An innocent misrepresentation renders the contract voidable – not void. What this means is that a contract has come into existence, is perfectly valid as a contract, and remains perfectly valid as a contract until such time as the misled party rescinds the contract, that is, ends the contract.

Of course, as with a breach of contract, the party misled can choose to affirm the contract, that is, carry on with the contract.

Rescission is usually the only remedy available to a person who has been misled by an innocent misrepresentation. An example of a misled party being able to rescind a contract is provided by *Redgrave v Hurd* (1881) (above).

12.12.3.2 Summary of remedies for misrepresentation

All misrepresentations make a contract **voidable** (as opposed to **void**) at the option of the misled person.

The misled person can:

- refuse to carry out his undertaking (available for both innocent and negligent misrepresentation)
- resist any claim for specific performance (available for both innocent and negligent misrepresentation) and
- claim damages (available only for negligent misrepresentation).

12.13 Summary

In this section you've seen:

- that a misrepresentation is not part of a contract. It is made before the contract is made. Really misrepresentation is the Tort of Deceit.
- that an operative misrepresentation consists of a false statement of existing or past fact made by one party before or at the time of making the contract, which is addressed to the other party and induces the other party to enter into the contract.
- that there must be some positive statement or conduct in order to amount to an operative misrepresentation.
- that there is no duty to disclose anything to the other party: see *Walters v Morgan* (1861).
- that a half-truth may be a misrepresentation: see *Dimmock v Hallett* (1866).
- that a mere silence is not a misrepresentation: see *Keates v Lord Cadogan* (1851).
- that a statement of opinion is not fact: see *Bisset v Wilkinson* (1927).
- that in certain circumstances a statement of opinion can constitute a representation of fact: see *Smith v Land & House Property Corp* (1884).
- that advertising 'puffs' are not representations of fact: see *Dimmock v Hallett* (1866).
- that the representation must be addressed to the party misled: see *Peek v Gurney* (1873).
- that although the representation must induce the contract, there is no need to prove that contract was made because of the representation: see *Smith v Chadwick* (1884).
- that the effect of misrepresentation is that the contract is voidable (as opposed to void) at the option of the misled person.
- that although we refer to negligent misrepresentation, it is more accurately referred to as 'misrepresentation under s 2(1) of the Misrepresentation Act 1967'.
- that the burden of proving that a person had 'reasonable ground to believe' the truth of their misrepresentation is a high one: see *Howard Marine & Dredging Co Ltd v Ogden & Sons (Excavations) Ltd* (1978).
- that an innocent misrepresentation is a misrepresentation where no element of fraud or negligence is present.

Chapter 13

Remedies for breach of contract

CONTENTS

13.1 Introduction

This chapter deals with what is meant by breach of contract and what are the effects of such a breach. We will see that not every breach of contract entitles the injured party to treat the contract as at an end and that in certain cases the injured party will have to go on with the contract and settle for monetary compensation – damages. In this chapter we will revisit conditions and warranties because the remedy available to the injured party will depend on what type of term has been broken. We will see that although damages are the normal remedy available to the injured party in certain cases the injured party will be able to treat the breach of contract by the other party as bringing the contract to an end. This chapter also shows that in order to get damages it must be shown that the loss was caused by the breach i.e. the loss must not be too remote. Finally, this chapter will show that damages are compensatory in nature and are not punitive or exemplary and in this context we will distinguish between penalty clauses and liquidated damages.

13.2 Breach of contract

13.2.1 Conditions and warranties revisited

In the terms of the contract section we saw that traditionally, all express terms in a contract were classified as either a condition or a warranty.

It was mentioned that this classification was important when it came to breach of a contract term by one of the parties to the contract.

If the term that was broken was a condition then the innocent party could, if they wished, accept the breach as bringing the contract would to end; they could also sue for damages.

If the term that was broken was a warranty then the innocent party could only sue for damages; the contract continued in existence.

> **WARNING!**
> You must be very careful to consider your actions if the other party has failed to perform their part of the contract.
>
> You must consider whether they have broken a condition or a warranty.
>
> If they have broken a **condition** then you can accept their breach and you can bring the contract to an end by informing them that you consider the contract as now at an end.
>
> **NB** You still have the right to sue for damages subject to what is said below.
>
> If, on the other hand, they have broken a **warranty**, you cannot treat that breach as giving you the right to treat the contract as at an end. Your only right is to sue for damages. You must continue with the contract.

13.3 Discharge at option of the injured party

Breach – even of a condition of a contract – does not itself terminate the contract (bring the contract to an end).

The injured party must elect (choose) to treat the contract as discharged; the injured party can choose to continue with (affirm) the contract: see *White & Carter (Councils) Ltd v McGregor* (1962).

But **remember** if the innocent party **does choose to affirm the contract** he still has his **right to sue for damages**.

NB In limited circumstances the innocent party has no choice but to treat the contract as discharged, for instance if he cannot carry out the contract without the cooperation of the other party e.g. a contract of employment.

13.4 Damages for breach of contract

13.4.1 Remoteness of damage

Damages are the normal remedy at common law for every breach of contract. In order to get damages it must be shown that the loss was caused by the breach.

However, the loss must not be too remote.

Hadley v Baxendale (1854)

Hadley, a mill owner, sued Baxendale, a carrier, for delay in delivering a broken mill shaft to the repairer. As a result of the delay Hadley's mill was idle for longer than he had anticipated and consequently his loss of profit was greater than anticipated. Baxendale admitted liability and offered to pay Hadley £25 damages. Hadley claimed extra damages for the loss he had suffered because of the extra delay.

The issue before the court was whether the **extra** damages claimed by Hadley were too remote.

The court held that the loss was too remote: that type of loss could not be foreseen by Baxendale.

Alderson B

We think the proper rule in such a case as the present is this:- where two parties have made a contract which one of them has broken, the damages which the other party ought to receive in respect of such breach of contract should be, either such as may fairly and reasonably be considered arising naturally, i.e., according to the usual course of things, from such breach of contract itself, or such as may reasonably be supposed to have been in the contemplation of both parties at the time they made the contract, as the probable result of the breach of it. Now, if the special circumstances under which the contract was actually made were communicated by the plaintiff to the defendant, and thus known to both parties, the damages resulting from the breach of such a contract which they would reasonably contemplate would be the amount of injury which would ordinarily follow from a breach of contract under those special circumstances, so known and communicated. But, on the other hand, if those special circumstances were wholly unknown to the party breaking the contract, he at the most could only be supposed to have had in his contemplation the amount of injury which would arise generally, and in the great multitude of cases not affected by any special circumstances, from such a breach of contract. For had the special circumstances been known, the parties might have especially provided for the breach of contract by special terms as to the damages in that case, and of this advantage it would be very unjust to deprive them . . .

Now, in the present case, if we are to apply the principles above laid down, we find that the only circumstances here communicated by the plaintiff to the defendant at the time the contract was made were, that the article to be carried was the broken shaft of a mill, and that the plaintiff was the miller of that mill. But how do these circumstances reasonably shew that the profits of the mill must be stopped by an unreasonable delay in the delivery of the broken shaft by the carrier to the third person? Suppose the plaintiff had another shaft in his possession put up or putting up at the time, and that he only wished to send back the broken shaft to the engineer who made it, it is clear that this would be quite consistent with the above circumstances, and yet the unreasonable delay in the delivery would have no effect upon the intermediate profits of the mill. Or, again, suppose that at the time of the delivery to the carrier the machinery of the mill had been in other respects defective, then also the same results will follow. Here it is true that the shaft was actually sent back to serve as a model for a new one, and that the want of a new one was the only cause of the stoppage of the mill, and that the loss of profits really arose from not sending down the new shaft in proper time, and that this arose from the delay in delivering the broken one to serve as a model. But it is obvious that in the great multitude of cases of millers sending off broken shafts to third persons by a carrier under ordinary circumstances such consequences would not in all probability have occurred, and these special circumstances were never communicated by the plaintiff to the defendant. It follows, therefore, that the loss of profit here cannot reasonably be considered such a consequence of a breach of contract as could have been fairly and reasonably contemplated by both these parties when they made this contract; for such loss would neither have flowed naturally from the breach of this contract in the great multitude of such cases occurring under ordinary circumstances, nor were the special circumstances, which perhaps would have made it a reasonable and natural consequence of such breach of contract, communicated to or known by the defendant.

13.5 Compensatory nature of damages

Damages are to put injured party into the position he would have been had the contract been performed. This can also include loss of profit.

Damages for breach of contract are **not** punitive or exemplary.

Damages are **compensation** for loss suffered – **not a punishment** for wrong inflicted.

If **no loss** has been actually suffered then only **nominal damages** (£2) will be awarded.

13.6 Duty to mitigate damage suffered

A person who has suffered loss from breach of contract must take any reasonable steps that are available to him to **mitigate the extent of the damage** caused by the breach.

He cannot claim to be compensated by the party in default for loss which is really **due not to the breach but to his own failure** to behave reasonably after the breach.

It is a question of fact in each case whether he has acted as a reasonable man might have been expected to act.

For example, you go into a high street TV shop and agree to buy a TV for £800 – a bargain at the price. The shop agrees to deliver it next Monday. Unfortunately, the shop has sold out of stock and cannot deliver the TV. An identical TV is on offer at two other high street TV shops. In one shop the TV is on sale for £900; in the other shop it is offer at £1,000. To mitigate your loss you must buy the set at £900 not £1,000. The damages you will be able to claim from the original TV shop is the difference between the price you agreed with them (£800) and the price you paid (£900) for the TV set, namely £100.

13.7 Penalty clauses and liquidated damages

13.7.1 Assessment of damages by the parties

Often a clause will be incorporated into the contract which **assesses the damages** at which the parties rate a breach of contract by one or both of them.

The clause **must** be a **genuine attempt** to assess damages – a **liquidated damages** clause – rather than a true **penalty** clause.

English Law **does not accept penalty clauses**!

Whether a clause is a **liquidated damages clause** or a **penalty clause** is a matter of construction judged at the time of making the contract.

13.8 Rules for ascertaining whether penalty or liquidated damages

In *Dunlop Pneumatic Tyre Co v New Garage and Motor Co* (1915) Lord Dunedin summarised the rules for ascertaining whether a clause was a penalty clause or liquidated damages clause.

Lord Dunedin

I shall content myself with stating succinctly the various propositions which I think are deducible from the decisions which rank as authoritative:–

(1) Though the parties to a contract who use the words 'penalty' or 'liquidated damages' may prima facie be supposed to mean what

they say, yet the expression used is not conclusive. The Court must find out whether the payment stipulated is in truth a penalty or liquidated damages.

(2) The essence of a penalty is a payment of money stipulated as in terrorem of the offending party; the essence of liquidated damages is a genuine covenanted pre-estimate of damage.

(3) The question whether a sum stipulated is penalty or liquidated damages is a question of construction to be decided upon the terms and inherent circumstances of each particular contract, judged of as at the time of the making of the contract, not as at the time of the breach.

(4) To assist this task of construction various tests have been suggested, which if applicable to the case under consideration may prove helpful, or even conclusive. Such are:

   (a) It will be held to be penalty if the sum stipulated for is extravagant and unconscionable in amount in comparison with the greatest loss that could conceivably be proved to have followed from the breach.

   (b) It will be held to be a penalty if the breach consists only in not paying a sum of money, and the sum stipulated is a sum greater than the sum which ought to have been paid . . .

   (c) There is a presumption (but no more) that it is penalty when 'a single lump sum is made payable by way of compensation, on the recurrence of one or more or all of several events some of which may occasion serious and others but trifling . . .'

On the other hand:

   (d) It is no obstacle to the sum stipulated being a genuine pre-estimate of damage, that the consequences of the breach are such as to make precise pre-estimation almost an impossibility. On the contrary, that is just the situation when it is probable that pre-estimated damage was the true bargain between the parties.

13.9 Limiting sum

A **liquidated damages clause clause** can act as a type of '**exclusion clause**' – not excluding liability but limiting liability; this the courts will accept provided it's a **genuine attempt** to assess damages.

Cellulose Acetate Silk Co Ltd v Widnes Foundry (1925) Ltd (1933)
Widnes Foundry contracted with the Silk Company to deliver and erect an acetone recovery plant. The contract stated that the work would be completed in 18 weeks. Clause 10 of the agreement stated:

If this period of 18 weeks is exceeded [Widnes Foundry] to pay by way of penalty the sum of £20 per working week for every week you exceed the 18 weeks.

Widnes Foundry was 30 weeks late in completing their work. The Silk Company sued Widnes Foundry for £5,850 which, they claimed, was the actual loss they had suffered through the delay. Widnes Foundry claimed that their liability was limited by clause 10 to £600 only.

If Clause 10 was a liquidated damages clause then Widnes Foundry's liability would be limited to £600.

If, on the other hand, Clause 10 was a penalty clause the court would strike it out of the contract and Widnes Foundry's liability would be £5,850.

The issue before the court was whether clause 10 was a liquidated damages clause or a penalty clause?

The court held that clause 10 was a liquidated damages clause.

Lord Atkin
What then is the effect of clause 10? . . . I entertain no doubt that what the parties meant was that in the event of delay the damages and the only damages were to be £20 a week, no less and no more. It has to be remembered that the Foundry Company's business in this respect was to supply an accessory to a large business plant for which they had no responsibility. The extent of the purchasers' business might be enormous; their expenses were beyond the sellers' control; and it would be a very ordinary business precaution for the sellers in such a case to say: 'we will name a date for delivery but we will accept no liability to pay damages for not observing the date; for if we were by our default to stop the whole of your business the damages might be overwhelming in relation to our possible profit out of the transaction. We won't incur any such risk.' This precaution the prospective sellers took in their printed Condition 10. They definitely negative any liability for delay. The purchasers have ample notice of this in the first quotation form sent to them on February 16. The purchasers pressed for an earlier date; they got it, and getting it without more they would still only have a business firm's assurance of delivery by that date; they would still be unable to claim damages from them for breach. The sellers ask for an addition to the price in order to enable them to give the earlier delivery; the buyers ask for some compensation if they do not get the delivery they want. It is agreed at £20 per week of delay. It appears to me that such sum is provided as compensation in place of the no compensation at all which would otherwise have been the result. Except that it is called a penalty, which on the cases is far from conclusive, it appears to be an amount of compensation measured by the period of delay. I agree that it is not a pre-estimate of actual damage. I think it must have been obvious to both the parties that the actual damage would be much more than £20 a week; but it was intended to go towards the damage, and

it was all that the sellers were prepared to pay. I find it impossible to believe that the sellers who were quoting for delivery at nine months without any liability, undertook delivery at eighteen weeks, and in so doing, when they engaged to pay £20 a week, in fact made themselves liable to pay full compensation for all loss.

For these reasons I think the Silk Company are only entitled to recover £20 a week as agreed damages.

Dunlop Pneumatic Tyre Co v New Garage and Motor Co (1915)

Dunlop entered into a contract with New Garage under which they supplied them with car tyres and tubes. By this contract New Garage bound themselves not to sell to any customer at prices less than the current price list issued by Dunlop. Clause 5 of the contract stated: 'we agree to pay to the Dunlop the sum of £5 for each and every tyre or tube sold or offered in breach of this agreement, as and by way of liquidated damages and not as a penalty.'

Dunlop discovered that New Garage had sold tyres and tubes at under the current list price and sued New Garage for damages. New Garage admitted the breach.

The issue before the court was whether the £5 fixed in the agreement a penalty clause or liquidated damages clause?

The court held that the £5 was a liquidated damages clause.

Lord Dunedin

Turning now to the facts of the case, it is evident that the damage apprehended by the appellants owing to the breaking of the agreement was an indirect and not a direct damage. So long as they got their price from the respondents for each article sold, it could not matter to them directly what the respondents did with it. Indirectly it did. Accordingly, the agreement is headed 'Price Maintenance Agreement,' and the way in which the appellants would be damaged if prices were cut is clearly explained in evidence by Mr. Baisley, and no successful attempt is made to controvert that evidence. But though damage as a whole from such a practice would be certain, yet damage from any one sale would be impossible to forecast. It is just, therefore, one of those cases where it seems quite reasonable for Parties to contract that they should estimate that damage at a certain figure, and provided that figure is not extravagant there would seem no reason to suspect that it is not truly a bargain to assess damages, but rather a penalty to be held in terrorem.

13.10 Summary

In this section you've seen:

- that when considering whether a clause in a contract is intended to be a penalty clause or a liquidated damages clause the words used to describe 'limiting clause' do not matter. 'Equity looks to the intent rather than the form': see *Cellulose Acetate Silk Co Ltd v Widens Foundry (1925) Ltd* (1933).

- that with rescission of a contract the old contract is brought to an end and is completely replaced with a new contract. With variation of a contract the original contract still exists, but some of the terms are varied.
- that a breach of contract by one party always entitles other to sue for damages. However, not every breach operates as a discharge – in other words not every breach entitles the innocent party to accept the breach and treat the contract as at an end. In order to have this effect the breach must be such as to constitute a repudiation by the party in default of his obligations under the contract.
- that breach of contract does not itself terminate the contract. The injured party must elect (choose) to treat the contract as discharged; he can choose to continue with (affirm) the contract: see *White & Carter (Councils) Ltd v McGregor* (1962).
- that if the innocent party to a breach of contract does choose to affirm the contract he still has his right to sue for damages.
- that English Law does not accept penalty clauses.
- that whether a clause is a liquidated damages clause or a penalty clause is a matter of construction judged at the time of making the contract: see *Dunlop Pneumatic Tyre Co v New Garage & Motor Co* (1915).

Index